GOLF'S FORGOTTEN LEGENDS

GOLF'S FORGOTTEN LEGENDS

LEGENDS

& Unforgettable Controversies

JEFF GOLD

NEW YORK

GOLF'S FORGOTTEN LEGENDS
& *Unforgettable Controversies*

© 2015 Jeff Gold.

Published in New York, New York, by Morgan James Publishing. Morgan James and The Entrepreneurial Publisher are trademarks of Morgan James, LLC. www.MorganJamesPublishing.com

The Morgan James Speakers Group can bring authors to your live event. For more information or to book an event visit The Morgan James Speakers Group at www.TheMorganJamesSpeakersGroup.com.

The cover image is of the Great Triumvirate, whom you'll be reading about. This image is available for purchase through www.printsellers.com

A **free** eBook edition is available with the purchase of this print book.

CLEARLY PRINT YOUR NAME ABOVE IN UPPER CASE

Instructions to claim your free eBook edition:
1. Download the BitLit app for Android or iOS
2. Write your name in **UPPER CASE** on the line
3. Use the BitLit app to submit a photo
4. Download your eBook to any device

ISBN 978-1-63047-301-3 paperback
ISBN 978-1-63047-302-0 eBook
ISBN 978-1-63047-303-7 hardcover
Library of Congress Control Number:
2014941980

Cover Design by:
Rachel Lopez
www.r2cdesign.com

Interior Design by:
Bonnie Bushman
bonnie@caboodlegraphics.com

In an effort to support local communities, raise awareness and funds, Morgan James Publishing donates a percentage of all book sales for the life of each book to Habitat for Humanity Peninsula and Greater Williamsburg.

Get involved today, visit
www.MorganJamesBuilds.com

Habitat
for Humanity®
Peninsula and
Greater Williamsburg
Building Partner

I dedicate this literary masterpiece to Johnny Miller.
Don't ask me why.

TABLE OF CONTENTS

INTRODUCTION

with a nod to Tom Lehman

I would like to begin with an unusual golf story involving a Detroit pawn shop owned by my good friend, Les Gold. He has a behemoth shop, used as the set for the reality TV show "Hardcore Pawn." Les is a hell of a tough negotiator. In one episode, a burly fellow brings in a complete set of slightly used pro-line golf clubs—four woods, nine irons, a putter, a golf bag and even a pull cart. Les offers him a whopping $15 for everything and the customer becomes enraged. Les keeps his cool and signals his 7-foot, 400-pound security guard who proceeds to pick the guy up, with his golf clubs and cart, and throw him out the door— reminiscent of the mighty King Kong!

That incident, although a bit extreme, gave credence to my contention that golf is a contact sport and furthered one of the missions of *Golf's Forgotten Legend* which is to dispel the misconception that golf is not a real sport. The fact of the matter is that golf requires considerable athleticism and constant of risk of injury for the many professionals who hit thousands of practice balls weekly. Sadly, Johnny Miller (see Chapter 12) suffered every injury possible on the golf course.

Minnesota golfers also face prohibitively cold climates. While I have spent the better part of my life in this state, I've never figured out why the hell people call it the Midwest. It's so fricken cold here in the winter time, it should be called the Frigid North. During the bitterly cold winter of 2014, the Twin Cities area had more than 40 days of sub-zero temperatures.

Despite our climate, Minnesota has produced a handful of highly talented golfers—Tom Lehman being the most successful of the bunch. I was fortunate to become friends with Tom long before he achieved success on the PGA Tour. His story is a true fairy tale. But first let me explain why I wrote this book.

It was my desire to produce a compelling golf story book, with a bit of humor and controversy to draw the attention of the golf world and shake it up— along with preserving history of some of the most prominent legendary figures in professional golf.

In my research I identified 12 great, major champion winning, golf legends who have become somewhat forgotten. In Chapter 13 you'll find a golf legend unheard of by most golfers today—yet arguably the most talented golfer who ever lived!

The material I've put together is controversial at times—even in the appendix. In one chapter, you'll find an old masters photo with a story behind it that is straight out of the "Twilight Zone." I adopted a no-holds-barred approach to *Golf's Forgotten Legends*. Having said that, I have tried to show respect for deserving, famous golfers, and stick up for those who may have been mistreated by the golf world.

Tom Lehman is one of those golfers due our admiration. As a serious golfer, Tom had the same misfortune I had growing up in cold Minnesota. Despite the fact that the North Star state has more golfers per capita than any other state in the country, few Minnesotans have succeeded on the PGA Tour.

The most amazing golf performance I have witnessed is the success Tom has achieved on the PGA Tour and Champions Tour, overcoming the disadvantage of the long winters of our home state. For years after turning pro in 1982, it looked unlikely that Tom would be an exception to Minnesota golfers' lagging success rate. He played on the PGA Tour with little success from 1983 to 1985. He spent the next five years struggling to make a living in the Asia and South Africa tours.

By 1989 Tom considered quitting pro golf and taking an offer to coach the University of Minnesota golf team. However, he turned it down when he learned that part of his job would include renting cross-country skis for people to use on the university golf course in the winter.

Tom's fortune changed when the Ben Hogan Tour was established in 1990. After four wins in two years on the Hogan Tour, Tom regained his PGA Tour card in 1991, by topping the Hogan Tour's Money List and achieving Player of the Year honors. Tom has enjoyed PGA Tour membership since and was named PGA Player of the Year in 1996. In that year he won The Open Championship along with the prestigious, year ending, PGA Tour Championship.

In total, Tom has had 31 professional wins to date, including five official PGA Tour titles. He has been the only golfer in modern history to play in the final group, during the final round, in four consecutive U.S. Opens. The fact that he went 0 for 4 in those Opens could be blamed, in large part, on his putting. In Ryder Cup competition, however, Tom has one of the greatest singles records of all time. In his three appearances, he is 3-0. Most amazingly, he never carded a single bogey in any of the three.

I'd like to dispel the rumor about Tom and the so-called "ugly incident" at Brookline in 1999. European Ryder Cup captains, Mark James and Sam Torrance accused Tom of instigating the premature jubilation on the 17th hole of the final day. The fact is that Tom was the fifth player to join in on the 42-second celebration and he never even set foot on the green. Thus, it was unfair to blame Tom for that slightly inappropriate incident.

Tom's career brightened when he hit 50 and joined the Champions Tour in 2009. By the end of 2012, Tom had won seven times, three in Champion Tour majors. He capped off 2011 and 2012 by winning the Charles Schwab Cup and Player of the Year honors. Tom was the only golfer in history to win Player of the Year honors on all three U.S. tours and the first golfer to win the Schwab Cup in back-to-back years. The 2012 victory is especially remarkable in that he also won the Schwab Cup Championship.

Tom's sense of humor is under-appreciated by most golf fans who only see him as a rather stoic, focused competitor. His stories about golf events he's played in with his wife, Melissa, are very funny—except for time she beat him. That had to have been a tough blow to his ego.

Nevertheless, Tom's is a golf legend in Minnesota and only needs one more Champions Tour major win to be eligible for induction into the World Golf Hall of Fame. I predict Tom will be the first Minnesotan to be inducted. Yet I don't believe he has received the full credit he deserves. I predict great things for him heading into 2015. For crying out loud, Tom, don't let me down!

Though Tom travels in bigger golf leagues than I do, we share our love of golf history and appreciation for the forgotten legends of the game, such as Harry Vardon—the subject of Chapter 1.

HARRY VARDON

Leader of the Great Triumvirate

Harry Vardon was golf's first superstar. He lived 66 years from May 9, 1870, to March 20, 1937—and along the way suffered bouts of tuberculosis, but did not let that take him down. He was the first pro to play in knickers, with fancy-topped stockings, a hard collar and tie, and tightly buttoned jacket, but still had great freedom of movement.

This forgotten golf legend is one of Britain's famed "Great Triumvirate" of golfers. The other two are J.H. Taylor and James Braid. Vardon won The Open Championship a record six times and won the U.S. Open. In comparison, Taylor and Braid each won five Open Championships.

Vardon was born in Grouville, Jersey, a Channel Island between the U.K. and France. As a child he didn't have a chance to play much golf, but showed a natural talent for it. He came from a large, poor family of six boys and two girls. His father worked as a gardener and discouraged Harry from playing golf. Harry never had a lesson but started taking a serious interest in golf at age 13, while

1

working as an apprentice gardener, and played successfully in a few tournaments in his late teens.

At age 20, he followed his 18-year-old brother to England and landed a job in Yorkshire as a greens keeper. Vardon hadn't considered making professional golf his livelihood until his brother Tom turned pro and was doing well in tournaments—persuading him to test his skills against the top pros in the U.K. and Europe. It came easy for him.

His technique

He developed a demanding practice routine, with numerous swing drills, using set-up and alignment aids. Only 155 pounds, at 5-feet 9-inches tall, he nevertheless had large hands that fit the club beautifully. Vardon possessed a calm and relaxed demeanor. Self-taught, he made effortless, upright swings he would use successfully and steadfastly—never making adjustments to them the rest of his life.

Vardon became renowned for a consistent repeating swing that was more upright than his contemporaries and a higher ball flight. This gave his approach shots greater carry and a softer landing. He picked the ball clean and took just the tiniest of divots. Vardon was possessed with a talent and method so impressive he was considered a shot-making machine in the primitive era of hickory shafts and gutta percha balls.

He allowed his left arm to bend as he reached the top of his backswing, and there was no muscular stress in his swing. "Relaxation, added to a few necessary fundamental principles," he said, "is the basis of this great game."

Vardon was famous for the "Vardon grip," an overlapping grip most popular among professional golfers. He actually took up this grip after Johnny Laidlay, a champion Scottish amateur player, invented it. In all fairness, the grip should be called the "Laidlay grip." On the other hand, Vardon was the superstar of his day who made the grip famous.

Within a few years of turning pro, Vardon became golf's first known star since the days of Young Tom Morris.

(The story of Young Tom Morris is every bit as tragic as it is astounding. He played during the ancient days of professional golf, when The Open

Championship consisted of just 36 holes—contested over three 12-hole rounds. He is the only golfer to win four consecutive Opens, starting in 1868 at the tender age of 17.

Despite the brevity of the tournament, Young Tom was known for blow-out victories. He won his second and third Open titles by 11 and 12 strokes, respectively. That is equivalent to winning by 22 and 24 strokes, under the 72-hole format that the tournament was increased to 1892. For a brief period he dominated his nearest rivals. However, at age 24, his wife and newborn baby died at childbirth. The grief was more than he could bear and he died just four months later of a broken heart—on Christmas Day.

However, I feel that Old Tom Morris lacked a bit of discretion by throwing a party the day after Christmas to celebrate his good fortune of (finally) having a chance to win the Open again, with Young Tom out of the picture.)

In 1896, Vardon he won his first Open Championship. He won it again in 1898, 1899, 1903, 1911 and 1914. He was second on four occasions. His record of six Open Championships still stands today. In 1900, he became golf's first international celebrity when he toured the United States, playing in more than 80 matches and capping it off with a victory in the U.S. Open at Chicago Golf Club. A portion of Vardon's remuneration for this exhibition tour came from Spalding for playing their new Vardon Flyer gutta purcha golf ball.

He was the joint runner-up of the 1913 U.S. Open—a historic event that was falsely depicted in Bill Paxton's movie, "The Greatest Game Ever Played." At the age of 50, Vardon led the 1920 U.S. Open by four strokes with only seven holes to play. It looked like he had an easy victory in the bag. However, due to a nasty change in the weather and a shaky putter he wound up finishing second to his close friend, Ted Ray.

During his career, Vardon won 62 golf tournaments, including one run of 14 in a row, a record likely to last forever. Harry was known for his accuracy and control with all clubs, the greatest ever seen. However, after winning The Open Championship for the third time in 1903, Vardon was struck down with tuberculosis. It put him out of commission and into sanitariums off and on until 1910—after which, the game that had come so naturally for Vardon would never be easy again.

In his prime, Vardon was virtually unbeatable

In the image above Vardon gets ready to nail his drive on the first hole of the 1903 Open, with Old Tom Morris looking on in the background. Vardon won by six strokes over his brother, Tom Vardon—earning him a whopping £50. Sadly, Harry was struck with tuberculosis a few months later. As great as his record was, he lost 13 of his prime playing years, eight to his illness and five to World War I.

Vardon complained that playing on the lusher turf conditions in the U.S. led him to bad habits. The wound-rubber Haskel ball everyone started using reduced his shot-making advantage over the field. Vardon had to have been one of the few golfers in history who mourned the demise of the gutta percha ball. He was used to the harder turf of a British Open course, where it was easy for him to pick the ball cleanly.

After Vardon's return to the game in 1910, he was plagued by the dreaded jerky yips—before the word was coined—from nerve damage to his right hand. Yet Vardon played in the U.S. Open in 1900, 1913 and 1920. In 1900, the event was played at the Chicago Golf Club, and he won by shooting 313 (79-78-76-80). Harry was also credited with winning 70 exhibition matches in 1900, touring the U.S. and Canada. In that year, Vardon only lost two head-to-head matches in singles play, becoming golf's first international celebrity.

Vardon's 1913 U.S. Open playoff loss to Ouimet— dispelling a 100-year-old myth

This victory was a nice accomplishment for Francis Ouimet. However, at 43, with his health issues, Vardon wasn't quite up to playing back-to-back 36-hole rounds in the miserable cold and rain that hit the Boston area that week in late September.

Much has been said, in the past 100 years, of how Ouimet, the underdog, scored an incredible upset victory over Harry Vardon. But that's a bunch of hogwash. Ouimet was *no* underdog! In that nasty weather, Ouimet's youth vs. Vardon's older age and ill health, Ouimet's win two months earlier in the Massachusetts Amateur, and the fact that the event was held on Ouimet's home course—all placed Vardon at a disadvantage to Ouimet.

Vardon was the true underdog to Ouimet in the 1913 U.S. Open. It was an amazing accomplishment that old man Vardon was able to keep up with young gun Ouimet for 72 holes, with odds stacked against him. The notion that Ouimet hadn't been playing much golf prior to the 1913 U.S. Open is ridiculous! The guy had to have played a lot of golf that summer in order to win the Massachusetts Amateur in July and make it to the quarter-finals of the U.S. Amateur in August.

Vardon was four strokes up on Ouimet after the first day (shooting 75, 72) and it was obvious Vardon was on track to win the tournament had the weather not turned bad. His dismal, un-Vardon-like scores of 78, 79 were clear evidence that Vardon had run out of gas and was still recovering from the tuberculosis. Ironically, Vardon's illness, forcing him to delay his trip to America, is what caused him to play in the cold, rainy New England fall in the first place.

After 72 holes, Vardon, Ouimet and Ray tied for first with a total score of 301 (+8). In the playoff, after the skies cleared, it didn't help Vardon much. The bad weather had weakened him. He virtually handed the U.S. Open playoff win to Ouimet. To Ouimet's credit, however, his playoff performance was nothing short of textbook.

No one else played worth a damn that week. Young Walter Hagen finished three strokes out of a tie for first at 304 (+11), after closing with an 80! The following year, Hagen would win the U.S. Open by just one stroke, closing with a 73 and finishing at 290 (+2) total. That was an 11-stroke improvement over the low 72-hole scores in 1913.

Vardon managed to get over that playoff loss in time for the next major – the 1914 Open Championship at Prestwick, Scotland. This was the year Vardon won his sixth and final Open, over J. H. Taylor by three shots. His win, interestingly, was aided by a cameraman who distracted Taylor on the fourth hole—which led to J.H. making a nasty triple bogey 7 while Vardon made par. Taylor wound up ballooning to an ugly 83 that final round—giving Vardon the chance to win The Open with an 80. However, Harry managed to avoid the dreaded snowman in shooting a 78 to collect the champion's first prize, still the insultingly tiny sum of $50.

Due to the outbreak of World War I, that was the last Open Championship held until 1920—meaning Harry (with precious few competitive years left) had no opportunity, in the next five years, to defend his title and score a seventh Open win. Nevertheless, Vardon's record remains intact after 100 years. Even Tiger Woods, with his reoccurring injuries, seems to have no clue how to win a major—which is surprising, considering how dominant he was for so long.

Harry played in the U.S. Open for the last time in 1920 at the Inverness Club. This was another Open victory that Vardon was cheated out of due to vicious weather. With just nine holes to go, 2 over par for the tournament up to that point, he had a four-stroke lead. Even a 4-over-par 40 on the final nine would have given him a total of 294, and a one-stroke victory. However, as Harry stood on the tee of the long 12th (or 66th hole of that Open) a horrific storm suddenly swept in off Lake Erie. It was too much for poor old Harry, having recently turned 50. Vardon wound up staggering in with a 42, in complete exhaustion. Not having played in the U.S. Open since 1913, this was his second time in a row when he had a comfortable lead in the U.S. Open, before barely losing it to the onset of nasty weather.

Vardon tied for second place, one stroke behind Ted Ray, missing a short putt on the final hole to force a playoff. Harry ended up at 8-over-par 296 (74-73-71-78). Had Vardon won that year, he would have become, by far, the oldest winner in the history of the U.S. Open. Instead, Hale Irwin holds that record, after winning his third Open at just 45.

In his later years, Harry dabbled in golf course architecture, designing several courses in England, along with teaching golf, and writing golf instruction books. He continued battling tuberculosis until his death, living in Totteridge, Hertfordshire, England. After he died, the PGA of America created the Vardon Trophy. It is awarded annually to the player on the PGA Tour with the year's lowest adjusted scoring average.

In 1974, Vardon was selected as an initial inductee into the World Golf Hall of Fame. His most prestigious medals, including those from his six British Open Championships, are on display in a tribute to him at the Jersey Museum. He was, unquestionably, the greatest golfer of the 19th century and is referred to as "the icon of golfing."

Quotes by Harry Vardon

"More matches are lost through carelessness at the beginning than any other cause."

"I'm the best and I'll thank you to remember that."

"To play well you must feel tranquil and a t peace."

"I have never been troubled by nerves in golf as I felt I had nothing to lose and everything to gain."

"Never concede the putt that beats you."

"A great deal of unnecessary golf is played in this world."

"If I get a hole-in-one it will be a day to remember."

"Don't praise your own good shots. Leave that function to your partner who, if a good sport, will not be slow in performing it."

"If your opponent is playing several shots in vain, attempting to extricate himself from a bunker, do not stand near him and audibly count his strokes. It would be justifiable homicide if he wound up his pitiable exhibition by applying his niblick to your head."

"The most successful way to play golf is the easiest way."

Golf writer Bernard Darwin on Harry Vardon: *"I do not think anyone who saw him play in his prime will disagree as to this, that a greater genius is inconceivable."*

Vardon's secret to distance—a bent left elbow?

This photo is taken from Harry Vardon's book, *The Complete Golfer*, published in 1905. It is considered golf's first great instruction book. His teachings were quite advanced for the day.

Vardon originated the vertical swing. But there's an unusual aspect to his swing that few understand. It's the secret to his distance. Harry was considered a long-ball hitter, despite being sickly.

You've probably heard a golfer should keep his or her left arm straight. All the pros teach that, right? Contrary to popular thinking, Vardon was able to maximize his power and distance by bending his left elbow. But there is a difference between what the pros are trying to prevent and what Vardon did. When most amateurs bend their left elbow, they over-swing at the top and lose control of the club head. On the way down they will straighten their arm, causing extra movement, and a split-second swing adjustment needs to be made, to compensate for a change in their swing plane. It's nearly impossible to time a swing plane adjustment like that with any consistency.

What Vardon did was something different. He maintained the bend in his left elbow until just before impact. John Jacobs, in his book *The 50 Greatest Golf Lessons of the Century*, compared Vardon's swing to throwing a Frisbee. Vardon used his left arm as a whip bent in the middle. He threw his left arm down the target line like a discus thrower, but on a more vertical plane. He would release it, like a discus, down through the ball. The origin of this strange-looking technique likely was due to his whippy wooden-shafted clubs that behaved in a rather peculiar manner.

Besides his bent left elbow, Vardon owed his success largely to an upright swing method that drastically changed the shape of the golf shot. The traditional style was to drive the ball as hard as possible, at a low a trajectory, maximizing distance but giving up control where the ball would come to rest. Vardon, by contrast, hit the ball high in the air so it would land more softly and stop much more quickly, with less bouncing and rolling. This, with an adjustment in his stance, enabled him to land the ball closer to the flagstick than golfers using the traditional method. Modern-day golfers like Jack Nicklaus and Tiger Woods copied that aspect of Vardon's technique—neither were shabby golfers. But, with his game currently in shambles, I'm not sure whether to say that Tiger *is* or *was* a great player.

Vardon's near miss with the Titanic

Vardon suffered a bout of tuberculosis in the spring of 1912. At the time, he had scheduled a promotional tour to America to sponsor a golf ball from a new company called Dunlap. Due to illness, he was forced to cancel his trip. Missed by most golf historians, the ticket he cancelled was on the Titanic! Vardon reportedly commented to close confidants that this was the first time tuberculosis saved his life. I'm guessing this was kept hush-hush so the golf world would not learn about his debilitating illness.

The cruise ship disasters don't stop there. In 1915, the *New York Times* reported Vardon was booked on the Lusitania to depart from the U.K. on May

17 for the U.S. Open at Baltusrol in New Jersey. But the Lusitania never made it to America. On May 7 the Germans torpedoed it, sinking the ship off the coast of Ireland with 1,198 passengers losing their lives. Fortunately for the golf world, none of those victims was named Vardon.

The image is reportedly a rare copy of Vardon's boarding pass for the R.M.S. Titanic. I'm quite certain you won't find this in any other golf history book. It feels strange to say, but I'm glad Harry took ill with tuberculosis in spring of 1912. Apparently it's the only thing that prevented him from becoming one of 1,518 casualties of that epic disaster. And Vardon would never have had a chance to win his sixth Open Championship.

My final thought on Vardon is this: Forget about Byron Nelson's record of 10 PGA Tour wins in a row. (If you read my upcoming book, you'll learn why I only credit Nelson with 10 in a row, rather than 11.) Harry Vardon won 14 professional tournaments in a row (40 percent more than I credit Nelson with) making Harry, by far and away, the all-time leader in consecutive professional tournament wins. Surely, this is a record that will last eternal!

Harry Vardon major Championship wins: seven
Tournament wins (partial list)
Major championships are shown in **bold**.

1893 Kilmacolm Tournament (Scotland)
1896 **The Open Championship**, Ganton Match Play (England)
1897 Scottish Open; Cumbria, Windermere, Cambridge Opens (England); Carnoustie Open (Scotland)
1898 **The Open Championship**, St. Nicholas Tournament (Scotland)
1899 **The Open Championship**
1900 **U.S. Open**
1903 **The Open Championship**
1906 World of Golf Gold Medal
1907 Cannes Tournament (France)

1909   PGA Medal (England)

1911   **The Open Championship**, Tooting Bec Cup (England), German Open, Montecarlo Open (France)

1912   World of Golf Gold Medal, News of the World Match Play

1914   **The Open Championship**, Prince of Wales Open

1915   PGA Medal (England), Lord Roberts Memorial (Scotland)

1919   Daily Tournament (England)

1920   Bramshoot Cup (U.S.)

1921   U.K. vs. U.S.

Chapter 2

JAMES BRAID

*Second member of
the Great Triumvirate
but in Vardon's shadow*

J**ames Braid** won his first golf tournament at age 8, and lived to 80, from Feb. 6, 1870, to Nov. 27, 1950. This forgotten golf legend was a Scottish professional and the second member of the Great Triumvirate, alongside Harry Vardon and John Henry Taylor. Like Taylor, he won The Open Championship five times and was a renowned and prolific golf course architect.

Braid was born in Earlsferry, Fife, Scotland and took up golf at an early age. Like Vardon, he grew up in humble circumstances. His father labored behind a plow in the farming town about 15 miles south of St. Andrews called Earlsferry. He wasn't a golfer and discouraged James from taking up the sport. Braid left school at 13 to become an apprentice landscaper, sneaking in rounds of golf when his travels permitted.

His game developed along with an interest in club making, and in 1893 he became a club maker in London. He turned pro three years later at 26 and became known for his long driving. His swing was described as being both powerful and graceful.

James typically won the open by large margins. At Muirfield in 1901, he began with a drive out of bounds at the first hole, but from there on he played superb golf to defeat Vardon by three strokes and Taylor by four. At St. Andrews in 1905, he sailed to a five-stroke victory over Taylor and again at Muirfield in 1906, he triumphed by four strokes over Taylor.

But while Vardon and Taylor were already winning Opens, Braid struggled mightily with his putting using a wooden-headed putter. He improved dramatically when he switched to an aluminum-headed putter in 1900 made by Mills of Sunderland that he acquired at the 1900 Open at St. Andrews. With that change in flat sticks, the tournament-winning floodgates opened for him. In fact, it Taylor once said, "I have yet to meet the player who could hole the 10-yard putts with greater regularity" than Braid. He won The Open in 1901, 1905, 1906, 1908 and 1910. This gave Braid five Open wins before either Vardon or Taylor. However, Braid retired at age 42, just two years later in 1912.

His finest performance came at Prestwick in 1908 when he shot the Open record of 291 to win by eight strokes over Tom Ball. That record stood until Bobby Jones shattered it by six strokes at St. Andrews in 1927. Braid finished runner-up to Taylor in 1909, but came back the next year at St. Andrews to win his fourth Open in six years by six strokes, this time over Alexander Herd.

Braid excelled in match play, winning the British PGA Match Play Championship four times in 1903, 1905, 1907 and 1911. In 1910 James won the French Open in one of his few attempts at that title. He was also runner-up in The Open Championship in 1897 and 1909. With great consistency, Braid's worst finish in The Open Championship from 1901-1910 was fifth.

Given the opportunity, Braid was good enough to have a serious chance of winning multiple U.S. Opens. Due to motion sickness, however, he never traveled far enough to play in the U.S.—making it impossible for him to attempt a major in America.

After retirement, Braid became head pro at Walton Heath where he remained the rest of his life, and his passion switched from golf to golf-course design. Back in those days when a pro golfer was no longer competitive, what the hell else was he going to do? Golf announcing? Probably not. He designed or re-designed a staggering some 200 courses throughout the U.K., including Carnoustie, Troon,

Prestwick and Ballybunion. If he tried he may have been able to come up with even sillier names than that.

Many of Braid's best courses were inland park tracks (as opposed to seaside links), and some of these courses contain the earliest known uses of the dogleg. Braid is believed to have invented the dogleg (far better than being the inventor of the dog track—an accurate term for most of the muni courses in the Twin Cities area).

Braid was a founding member of the British PGA and authored an instructional book entitled *Advanced Golf*. That book may be a tad outdated today in how it discusses proper ways to use the niblick.

James Braid Open Championship wins: five
Tournament wins: 15

1901	The Open Championship (three strokes over Harry Vardon)
1902	Tooting Bec Cup
1903	News of the World Match Play, Tooting Bec Cup
1904	Tooting Bec Cup
1905	The Open Championship (five strokes over J.H. Taylor), News of the World Match Play
1906	The Open Championship (one stroke over Vardon)
1907	News of the World Match Play, Tooting Bec Cup
1908	The Open Championship (eight strokes)
1910	The Open Championship (four strokes), French Open
1911	News of the World Match Play
1920	British vs. America Match

CHAPTER 3

J.H. TAYLOR

*Third member of
the Great Triumvirate
also in Vardon's shadow*

J ohn Henry "J.H." Taylor was born March 19, 1871, in the village of Northam, Devon, England, to a family too poor to feed him and he was orphaned as a boy. But at age 11, he went out on his own and was hired as a caddie and greens-keeping assistant at the Royal North Devon Golf Club (later known as Westward Ho!). He caught on to greens keeping quickly and that led to golf-course design work in his later years.

This forgotten golf legend turned pro at 19, and worked at several different clubs before settling in at the Royal Mid-Surrey (RMS) Golf Club in 1899. He stayed at Mid-Surrey until he retired in 1946 at 74.

He was the longest living member of the fabled Great Triumvirate, with Harry Vardon and James Braid. Taylor won The Open Championship five times, his first two in 1894 and 1895 before he came to RMS, then another three in 1900, 1909 and 1913 as the RMS pro. He gained a reputation for blowing away the field in Open competition, winning each of his five championships by an average of six strokes. He also won the French and German Opens.

It was three-time Open Championship runner-up, Andrew Kirkaldy, who first admired the greatness of John Henry Taylor at age 20. After losing a challenge match to Taylor in 1891, Kirkaldy went back to St. Andrews and announced, "That young Englishman who just defeated me will win many Open Championships. You'll see more of Taylor. And then you'll know why he beat me, and why he will beat all the best of the day."

Kirkaldy proved to be right, of course. Three years after defeating Kirkaldy, JH became the first Englishman to win the Open. Taylor's accuracy was legendary. At Sandwich, where he won his first Open by five strokes in 1894, he would have the directional posts removed from the blind holes out of concern that his drives would strike them and ricochet into bunkers. The following year, he won by four shots over Sandy Herd at St. Andrews, with Kirkaldy six shots further back in third place.

"The mon's a machine," Kirkaldy said. "He can dae naething wrang." Vardon came along to dominate the Open from 1896-99, winning it three out the four years. However, Taylor returned to form in 1900 at St. Andrews in dominant fashion—Pulling away from the field after every round, he cruised to an easy eight stroke win over Vardon, with Braid 13 back in third place. Later in the year, he finished second to Vardon in the U.S. Open at Chicago Golf Club—that would end up being Taylor's one and only trip to the U.S.

In 1913 JH had another eight stroke blowout win—this time over Ted Ray at Hoylake. This latter tied Taylor with Braid and Vardon with five Open victories and was considered his most satisfying win since it came in horrendous conditions. In heavy wind and rain, Taylor pulled his cap down over his eyes, stuck out his chin, and anchored his large boots to the ground to maximize control over his compact swing. Nineteen years after his first Open victory, Taylor shot 304 to win easily cruise past Ray, the defending champion. JH's final round 79 must have seemed good to Ray who finished with an 84.

Taylor was very competitive as late as 1924 when he finished fifth at age 53 in The Open at Hoylake (won by Walter Hagen). In 1926 (the year Bobby Jones won his first Open) he managed to tie for 11th place at 55. However, as he used to boast, if the qualifying rounds were included, he was the lowest scorer of the week—an accomplishment for a man in his mid-50s in those days.

During Taylor's time, professional golfers earned the bulk of their money playing in exhibition and challenge matches, which required J.H. to spend most of his time away from Royal Mid-Surry.

Taylor's five Open victories all took place before World War I—followed by the five years The Open went dark. He was captain of the 1933 Great Britain Ryder Cup team that beat the United States and remains the only captain on either side to never play in the matches.

Taylor played the game very seriously, like Hogan, or vise-versa. JH once wrote: "To try to play golf really well is far from being a joke, and lightheartedness of endeavor is a sure sign of eventual failure." Bernard Darwin, who was a close friend, recalled that nobody, not even Bobby Jones, suffered more over championships than Taylor did. "Like Bobby," said Darwin, "(Taylor) had great control and might appear outwardly cool, but the flames leaped up from within."

Taylor was involved in the design of more than a half-dozen courses across England, starting in 1907. He's credited with developing and designing the first two public golf courses, still operating today in the Richmond Park area. He was president of Royal Birkdale, where he assisted in course design work. In 1949 at 77, he was given an honorary membership in Scotland's Royal & Ancient Golf Club of St Andrews (R&A).

Taylor, like Braid, was credited for inventing the dogleg. Apparently, they invented it about the same time and both men took credit for it. There should have been an 18-hole playoff between those two to determine which should take full dogleg credit. On second thought, based on their ages, sudden death may have been the better way to go.

Most of Taylor's later life was dedicated to teaching, writing books, making clubs and designing courses (including several local ones). J.H. wrote several golf books considered exceptional. Today, first editions of these books are sought after by collectors and worth hundreds of dollars. The clubs which he made with partner George Cann were of high quality for their time and in demand throughout the world. Even today, those clubs are sought after by collectors.

In 1901, Taylor was a co-founder and the first chairman of the British Professional Golfers' Association (with James Braid). This was the first association for professional golfers in the world. Bernard Darwin wrote that Taylor "had turned a feckless company into a self-respecting and respected body of men." Taylor also founded the Artisan Golfers Association and the Public Golf Course Association.

Golfers today, especially Americans, take for granted the foundations of modern golf that were developed more than a century ago—not knowing they have J.H. Taylor to thank. It's high time J.H. receives due credit.

He lived until Feb. 10, 1963, dying shortly before his 92nd birthday—an unusually long life for someone born in the 1870s. His death marked the end of the era which gave rise to the first "Big Three" of the golf world. He was the last of golfing greats from the 1800s.

J.H. Taylor Open Championship wins: five
Tournament wins: 14

1891	Challenge Match Play (England)
1894	**The Open Championship**
1895	**The Open Championship**
1900	**The Open Championship**
1901	Tooting Bec Cup
1904	News of the World Match Play
1908	**French Open, News of the World Match Play**
1909	**The Open Championship**, French Open
1912	**German Open**
1913	**The Open Championship**
1921	Roehampton Invitation
1929	Dutch Open

The Great Triumvirate

Here we have the famous English/Scottish golf pros who comprised the Great Triumvirate—James Braid, Harry Vardon and J.H. Taylor. What nice three-piece suits and ties these guys have on. That attire must have been mighty comfortable to play golf in. Is it just me, or do you think these stoic men look a lot more like funeral directors (with Scottish caps on) than professional golfers? I can just see each of them saying, "My condolences, ma'am, on the loss of your husband."

Nevertheless, these men were truly the "Big Three" of their time. May their memory live on forever!

CHAPTER 4

WILLIE ANDERSON
Great talent, short life

I n the 16 years spanning from the first U.S. Open golf championship to the first native-born American who actually won The Open—the English and Scottish prevailed. Native Scotsman **Willie Anderson** was said to be the best of the lot.

Willie Anderson (left) poses here with his close friend, Alex Smith. Anderson won the U.S. Open in 1901, 1903, 1904 and 1905 while Smith won it in 1906 and 1910 (beating 18-year-old Johnny McDermott in a playoff, for his second win—read all about Johnny in the next chapter.)

Willie Anderson, ah yes, this forgotten golf legend did well, but got a bad rap—almost as bad as that of Johnny McDermott. While McDermott is known as the forgotten American hero, Willie Anderson is the forgotten son of a small Scottish community that produced dozens of legendary golfers. In his short life, Willie Anderson compiled a record second to none, writes Francis R. S. Broumphrey, "but circumstance conspired to make this first great American almost forgotten."

There are a lot of nasty falsehoods about Anderson floating around, but my friend Douglas Seaton from Scotland, Willie Anderson's biographer, has the story down pat. I defer to him for much of Anderson's story, adding some tidbits I learned from another friend, Bill Kelly, author of *Birth of the Birdie—The First 100 Years of Golf at Atlantic City Country Club.*

Willie Anderson was born Oct. 21, 1879, across from the Abbey Church, in North Berwick, East Lothian, Scotland, reports Seaton. He was educated at the public school in North Berwick and was a licensed caddie on the West Links at the age of 11. Upon leaving school he apprenticed as a club maker under Alex Aitken in Gullane.

From Scotland to America

"Willie Anderson, aged 16 years, sailed for America on the S.S. Pomeranian from Glasgow," writes Seaton, "arriving at Ellis Island in March 1896...to take up his position at Misquamicut Golf Club, Watch Hill on Rhode Island and the famous amateur Horace Hutchinson considered Anderson to be one of the best."

Anderson extended the course at Misquamicut to 18 holes. Willie Park Jr. laid the first nine the previous year. Anderson then moved to Lakewood Golf Club in New York. In his first U.S. Open, in September 1897, Anderson finished second, one stroke behind Joe Lloyd after Lloyd eagled the 72nd hole—an amazing accomplishment for Willie, considering he was only 17 at the time.

A golf pro at 10 clubs in 14 years, Willie Anderson worked at Baltusrol and Montclair, New Jersey, Apawamis Country Club in New York, and St. Louis Country Club.

"Willie's father and brother emigrated in 1900 and when Willie left Montclair Country Club in 1902 his father took over as a resident professional," writes Seaton. Jerry Travers was a member at Montclair when he won the U.S. Amateur in 1907 and 1910 and the U.S. Open in 1915.

Tom Anderson Sr. remained at Montclair until his death in 1913. Willie's younger brother, Tom Anderson Jr., also worked at Montclair in the 1909-10 season and as head pro in 1913-15. Willie's mother Jessie remained in Edinburgh, Scotland, with her four daughters.

"During the winter months Anderson was a pro at St. Augustine in Florida (now home of the World Golf Hall of Fame). In December 1899, Anderson traveled west playing in exhibition matches with U.S. Open champion Horace Rawlins. To earn some money Anderson and Rawlins worked as greens keepers at Oakland Golf Club, San Francisco. They entered the Southern California Open at Coronado Beach which Anderson won by one stroke from Alex Smith.

"In the 1900 U.S. census, Willie Anderson was listed as a boarder living with a European couple in the town of Oconomowoc, Wisconsin.

"At the 1901 U.S. Open played at Myopia Hunt Club near Boston, Willie Anderson and Alex Smith posted 72-hole scores of 331, to tie the tournament. In the first 18-hole playoff in Open history, which had to wait until the Monday because Sunday was members' day at Myopia, Anderson won by one stroke.

"At that championship, the American media picked up on Anderson's quote when he growled, 'No, we're no goin' tae eat in the kitchen' ," setting the tone for the other golf professionals, notably Walter Hagen, who refused to live by the outdated social standards that did not give golf professionals access to the dining room. Willie was furious when told professionals could not enter the clubhouse. The players were eventually allowed to eat in a specially erected tent.

"At Christmas 1901, Anderson traveled to California where he was engaged in giving golf lessons at the Hotel Green in Pasadena. Anderson was described as sturdy, with muscular shoulders, brawny forearms and exceptionally large hands. His accuracy was legendary, particularly with his favorite club, the mashie, equivalent to the present-day five iron.

"He drove the ball more off his left than his right foot, hitting it 233 yards. The strongest part of his game was his brassie, particularly from a bad lie, and he changed to the overlapping grip in 1900. His grip was more of an interlock than that of the Laidlay-Vardon-Taylor school, for the index finger of his left hand extended through between the third and little fingers of the right, instead of allowing only the knuckly to show in the aperture. His was not the upright swing of Vardon, but the flatter, fuller sweep of the typical Scot.

"Anderson regularly played with eight clubs: driver, brassie, cleek, midiron, one he called a pitching iron, heavy-centered mashie, large mashie-niblick, and putting cleek. He named the driver as his favorite; then the mashie, midiron and brassie."

Willie Anderson also hit blindfolded, sometimes as many as 20 balls at a time, a practice picked up by his friend and mentor Chick Evans, a great local amateur. "Described as a dour man who attended strictly to business and displayed little sense of humor on the course," writes Seaton, "Anderson …was a mixer off the course and popular with his fellow professionals…Willie's unhurried move through the ball disguised effortless power. He was also a rhythmical putter but his main attribute was his unflappable demeanor."

Willie's style

"Golfers during Anderson's time essentially wore clothes formal enough to attend church in, but not Willie Anderson. His typical attire was a tartan wool cap pulled low (to camouflage his large ears), baggy plaid shirt, cloth neckerchief (instead of a silk tie), and an old tweed jacket," according to Seaton.

There is a classic golf photo of some early professional golf champions sitting under a tree, surrounded by caddies and young kids. Willie Anderson is the fellow in the middle, his odd unstuffy dress a new sporting style for players.

"In 1902, Anderson was resident pro at Hotel Raymond in Pasadena, California, and on the 17th September 1902 captured his first Western Open, then a major, shooting a record 299 for 72 holes with one round of 69. Anderson became the first player to hold the titles to the U.S.'s two major tournaments, and no golfer had previously broken 300 for 72 holes in America.

"In October, the U.S. Open was played at the Garden City Golf Club," notes Seaton, "where Willie finished fifth, and the new Haskell rubber-cored ball was now in use. The 1903 U.S. Open was played at Baltusrol in New Jersey where Anderson was the pro in 1898….In the 1903 playoff for the U.S. Open, which was marred by pouring rain, Anderson beat David Brown by two strokes, 82-84. Willie Anderson became the first two-time winner of the Western Open on 1st July 1904 with a four-stroke victory over Alex Smith…. One week later at the U.S. Open played over Chicago's Glen View Course, Willie didn't need a playoff this time as he prevailed by five strokes, setting a U.S. Open record of 303, and his closing round 72 was also an 18-hole tournament record.

"Anderson designed clubs for Worthington Manufacturing and endorsed the 'near indestructible' Champion ball. Their woods bearing his signature were the first example of an autograph brand club in America.

"In June 1905, Willie Anderson and Alex Smith returned to Scotland especially to take part in The Open Championship at St Andrews. Smith finished 16th but Anderson's performance was disappointing, taking 86 and 88 for the first two rounds and failing to qualify."

When one golfer asked how Will Anderson played out of bunkers, " 'he was never in them,' the response came, a fact we now know to be wrong," Seaton notes.

"Willie struggled with the new bunkers at St Andrews; he was in eight of them in the first round. The bunkers were laid out by one of his father's apprentice greens keepers for North Berwick, Hugh Hamilton. He took over from Tom Morris as head greens keeper and was responsible for creating many of the bunkers at St Andrews and lengthened the course in reaction to the Haskell ball. The newspapers reported that Willie Anderson was dressed in a grey jersey and blue trousers and the headlines suggested he must be the first golfer dressed like that to drive off the first tee at St Andrews.

"Anderson and Smith returned to the states in September for the U.S. Open at Myopia Hunt Club near Boston. At first, it looked as if Anderson was out of the running for the third straight title. Scores of 81 and 80 left him five strokes behind Alex Smith and Stewart Gardner. But...by the 70th hole, he had a four-stroke lead and held it together to prevail by two over Smith. Anderson received $200, a gold medal and custody of the cup was given to the club.

"The eastern Professional Golfers Association was established in 1905 following a meeting held in the luxury Astor House Hotel, New York, where more than 70 pros attended including George Thompson, and Willie Anderson was elected to the Executive Committee.

"In March 1906, Willie escorted his wife back to the U.S.A. where he had signed a contract at Onwentsia Country Club, Illinois, which was reported to be for more money than any other golf pro in the U.S.A.

"In 2006, Mike Marshall, the historian at Apawamis Country Club, discovered that Willie Anderson's wife Agnes was born in 1883, the daughter of an Irish immigrant John Beakley and his wife Mary. Agnes was a native of Rye, Westchester, New York and they met while Willie was pro at Apawamis.

"On 18th June 1908, at Normandie Park Golf Club in St. Louis, Anderson became the first three-time winner of the Western Open…and the 15th September 1909 Willie won the Western Open at Skokie Golf Club in Illinois, for the fourth time.

"Tom Mercer, a fellow pro and close friend of Anderson, said that although Willie was not a glad-hander, he went that route with his friends, buying them drinks and probably his convivial habits had much to do with his undermining health.

"In 1910, Anderson returned from his winter post in Florida which he had for the previous six years, to take up the position of head pro at the Philadelphia Cricket Club, venue for the U.S. Open in June."

It was at this U.S. Open that a young Philadelphia caddie, the teenage son of a postal clerk, tied for the lead and faltered at the end of the Scottish professionals. His father was surprised to read about his son the next day in the newspapers. Johnny McDermott would come back to win the next two U.S. Opens back-to-back, and become the first native-born American and, at 19, still the youngest to have won The Open. And like Willie Anderson, McDermott would be touted as possibly the best-ever player of the game, but whose career would be cut dramatically short.

Going down hill

"It was reported in some quarters that Anderson's game had deteriorated but he was still playing to a high standard," writes Seaton. "In April 1910 he was second in the Florida Open, played several challenge matches with Gilbert Nicholls, described in the press as being of an excellent standard. In July he was a finalist in the Eastern Professional Golfers Association tournament. He did not show to defend his Western Open title at the end of August which may have been a reflection on his health."

There's a photo of Willie Anderson and Gil Nicholls together on the day before Anderson died. Nicholls was one of the old pros who played well in early tournaments, and I believe, held the first professional's job at Seaview, only to be replaced by Scottish pro James "Jolly Jim" Fraser, when Nicholls had a run-in with Seaview club owner Clarence Geist.

"Exhibitions were still where Anderson made most of his money and in October he traveled to the Pittsburgh area for three 36-hole matches with other leading pros and amateurs," writes Seaton. "On 24th October, the day after he and Gil Nicholls lost on the last hole to amateurs Eben Byers and William Fownes, Anderson returned to his home on Wissachkon Avenue, Chestnut Hill, near Philadelphia where he died the following day at age 31.

"On 28th October 1910, Willie Anderson was buried in Ivy Hill cemetery in Philadelphia. His father and mother attended the funeral. Three years later, Willie was followed to the grave by his father Tom, age 59, after 13 years as pro at Montclair Golf Course in New Jersey. Beside them is a statue of a golfer erected by the Eastern Golfers Association, whose president at the time was Jack Hobens, the former North Berwick caddie.

"Following Anderson's death, the amateur golfer Chuck "Chick" Evans Jr., twice U.S. Amateur Champion, collaborated with businessman C.B. Lloyd of The Goodrich Company to raise funds for Willie Anderson's widow. They organized a special exhibition of moving pictures of noted golfers at the Chicago Indoor Golf School, with all proceeds going towards the fund." It would be interesting to find out what happened to these early "moving pictures of noted golfers."

You can't read a story about Willie Anderson that doesn't tell you he died young from drinking too much, but that story doesn't hold water. For one, there are only a few references of him drinking at all, and one report seems to get all the play. In addition, he couldn't have kept up his high standards of play if he was an alcoholic and drank himself to death, as reported in widely published accounts.

"It was reported in some quarters that Anderson died of arteriosclerosis, a fatal hardening of the arteries," writes Seaton. "The *Philadelphia Public Ledger* said he suffered a brain tumor. Other sources suggest Anderson may have died from something less socially acceptable—acute alcoholism. Most modern descriptions of Anderson—'dour' personality and 'boozy' lifestyle seem to emanate solely from one man quoted in one place—in a profile of Anderson in the December 1929 issue of *The American Golfer*. In 2005, however, golf writer Bill Fields searched the Philadelphia city archives and discovered the official cause of death for the 31-year old Anderson wasn't hardening of the arteries, as has long been reported, but epilepsy."

You can't help but feel sorry for poor Willie. Today, that's a very treatable condition.

Redeemed by history

Willie was inducted into the World Golf Hall of Fame in 1975 and it described him, as he was noted by others before, as "a sturdy man, with muscular shoulders, brawny forearms and exceptionally large hands. He played with a flat, full-sweeping action that was characteristic of the Scots and known as the 'St Andrews swing.' Despite what many considered to be swing flaws, Anderson was consistently accurate." Anderson carried only eight clubs, but he was equally adept with each of them.

Willie Anderson was the first person to win four U.S. Opens. He won those four in just five years, 1901-1905. Three of them (1903-05) were won in succession, making Anderson the only golfer to win three U.S. Opens in a row. He also won four Western Opens (1902, 1904, 1908, 1909), an event that was the second-biggest pro event in the U.S. at the time. In addition to his great U.S. Open record, he was highly sought after as a golf instructor.

Scottish-American golfer Fred McLeod (winner the U.S. Open in 1908 and close friend of Willie's) once commented, "Anderson at his best was as good as Walter Hagen or Bobby Jones." That tells me Willie was mighty damn good.

Seaton told me he was pleased that my book dispels old rumors of Willie as an alcoholic because they caused a great deal of harm to his reputation. Added Seaton, "During the winter of 1908, Fred McLeod joined Anderson and several other pros in California. McLeod was raised in a family where alcohol was strictly forbidden, and his father was manager of the Temperance Café in North Berwick. Living with Anderson for eight weeks in California, if there was any mention of alcohol, McLeod would not have taken part. Also, Chick Evans would not have allowed himself to be associated with Anderson if the alcohol-related stories were true.

"An extract in *The Yonkers Statesman*, Philadelphia, May 27, 1930, states that the Willie Anderson Memorial Cup was organized among his fellow professionals and played over the Flourtown course of the Philadelphia Cricket Club. The North Berwick pros who gathered from all over the U.S.A. to remember Willie Anderson and enjoy the company of old friends included Fred McLeod, Jack Hobens, George Thomson, Jack Campbell and Jim Ferguson. The Memorial Cup was won by George McLean, 73, from Yonkers, New York, a member of the United States Ryder Cup Team, and McLeod was second. If Anderson was an alcoholic, as suggested in some quarters, would all those taking part for more than 20 years support the Memorial Cup?

"Also among the list of players in 1930 was a Willie Anderson pro at Powelton Club, Newburgh (Balmville), New York. Could this be Willie Anderson's son?" That makes sense to me, as he would have been in his 20s by then.

Seaton writes of other famous North Berwick, Scotland golfers, as well. Many thanks to Douglas for all the research and writing he's done, a great deal of which can be found on his website at www.northberwick.org.uk/anderson.html.

William Law Anderson is still the only man to win three consecutive U.S. Open titles, and only Bobby Jones, Ben Hogan and Jack Nicklaus have equaled his total of four championships. (Hogan actually won five U.S. Opens, counting his 1942 Open win during the year they called it the *Hale America Open*—in commemoration of the U.S. entry into World War II.)

His first significant win came in 1899 at the Southern California Open, before he started reeling off U.S. Open wins. In the 14 straight Opens that he played, Anderson won four, was second once, third once, fourth twice, fifth three times, 11th twice and 15th once. He won titles with both the old gutta-percha ball and the rubber-cored ball, which was invented in 1902.

Anderson was known for being accurate with every club in his bag—all eight of them. That consistency combined with being a great pressure player, made him a mighty tough foe with talent that was highly respected.

Willie Anderson major championship wins: four
U.S. Open: 1901, 1903, 1904, 1905

Western Open Championship wins: four
1902, 1904, 1908, 1909 (similar in status to a major, in those days)

CHAPTER 5

JOHNNY MCDERMOTT

America's first golf hero

He was destined for stardom until succumbing to severe depression early in life. If that wasn't bad enough, in recent times he was maligned by both *Golf Magazine* and the movie "The Greatest Game Ever Played." Sadly, Johnny is the most disrespected legendary golfer in the history of the game.

John J. McDermott Jr. was born in Philadelphia Aug. 12, 1891, and died Aug. 1, 1971, at age 79. But McDermott died inside at the tender age of 22, in 1914, when his life unraveled to such an extent it made Tiger Woods's fall from grace in 2009 seem like a joy ride. Nevertheless, Johnny was one of the world's top players from 1910 and 1914.

This forgotten golf legend was the first American golfer to beat the Brits. He won the U.S. Open in 1911 and 1912, and remains the youngest-ever champion of that event, at age 19. At 18 he tied for first in the 1910 U.S. Open, before losing in a playoff to Alex Smith. In the 1912 U.S. Open they played in rain and thunderstorms. McDermott hit two drives out of bounds in his third round, yet managed to card a round of 74. A solid final round of 71 enabled him to defend his Open crown by two strokes.

These U.S. Open victories followed his winning the Philadelphia Open in 1910 over Willie Anderson. Tying the Smith brothers for the national championship that same year, McDermott looked forward to the 1911 U.S. Open with confidence. He told others in the Atlantic City locker room that "the foreigners are through." Leaving the clubhouse he turned to his assistant, saying, "You're carrying the clubs of the next Open champion." And he lived up to his word.

At the 1911 U.S. Open at the Chicago Golf Club, McDermott missed an opportunity to take the championship outright and faltered into a three-way playoff with Mike Brady and George Simpson for the title, with a total of 307. Because of the "Blue Laws" the playoff was not held until Monday. It is well known that McDermott won the playoff, becoming the first American born golfer to win the U.S. Open, and also the youngest, but here is the rest of the story.

Before the playoff began, a representative from the St. Mungo Mfg. Co. told the three players that the company would match the $300 first place prize if the winner was playing one of their Colonel golf balls. McDermott agreed to change from the Rawlings Black Circle ball to a Colonel ball. On the first hole, McDermott's first two tee shots went out-of-bounds. With his third tee shot he made a birdie four for a score of six. The out-of-bounds penalty at that time was loss of distance only. McDermott also made a bogey on the third hole, but when he holed a short putt for a birdie four on the last hole, he was the United States Open Champion, and $600's richer. By doing so he became the first and youngest American-born champion.

"He ended the domination of immigrant British golfers," wrote Robert Sommers, in his book, *The U.S. Open: Golf's Ultimate Challenge,* "and was leading a wave of young home-breds…who were to revolutionize the way the game was played….McDermott's victory had not only shown that American-born golfers could outplay the best of the imports, it also quickened interest in The Open."

A record 131 players entered the 1912 Open at the Country Club of Buffalo, where McDermott defended his title, firing rounds of 74, 75, 74 and 71 which gave him a 294 total, and yet another first—to score under par over 72 holes.

McDermott won The Open twice before he reached 21, and was being compared to four-time Open winner Willie Anderson. "There seemed to be no limit to what he might accomplish," wrote Sommers. "He was doing well financially: clubs were marketed under his name, he endorsed balls, played $1,000 exhibition matches, gave lessons, and invested his money. The world was a lovely place."

"To our off-side way of thinking," sports writer Grantland Rice said, "John was the greatest golfer America had ever produced, amateur or professional, when it came to a combination of nerve, coolness and all-around skill from the tee to the green. McDermott had no weakness in any part of his game and, what is more to the point, he was pretty sure to be at his best under the heaviest fire. Furthermore, his fortunes appeared to take a turn for the better at the 1913 British Open when he finished fifth overall, the first time an American broke into the top British ranks. Then fate would deal McDermott a cruel hand."

In 1913 McDermott held many crowns—he was the two-time defending U.S. Open champion and he had won the Western Open, then a major tournament, and all roads were leading toward the 1913 U.S. Open at the Country Club at Brookline, Massachusetts. Golf fans greatly anticipated the showdown between McDermott and the great British pro Harry Vardon, on tour in the states.

Before Brookline however, Vardon and Ted Ray entered a tournament at Shawnee-on-the-Delaware, which attracted nearly the same field as the U.S. Open. McDermott won easily, shooting eight strokes better than runner-up Alex Smith, and 13 strokes better than Vardon. McDermott was the only one in the field to break 300 with a 292.

Damned in the press

In the course of victory McDermott was lifted into the air and made a quick speech, although what he said verbatim has been lost in the retelling of the tale. In the New York papers, McDermott was quoted as saying, "We hope our foreign visitors had a good time, but we don't think they did, and we are sure they won't win the National Open."

McDermott was not aware that he had offended anyone and when he was told otherwise, he tried to apologize. "I am broken-hearted over the affair," McDermott said, "and the way the papers used my speech. No harm was meant and I am certainly sorry that my talk has been taken up by this manner." But the New York press and the British reporters played it up to the point in which the 1913 U.S. Open would be covered by more than just sports writers and golf would break onto the front page once again.

Golf course architect A.W. Tillinghast later said that both Englishmen accepted the apology, "because they realized Johnny was flush with victory, young and comparatively uneducated." The older men may have been understanding, but others were not so forgiving. In his defense McDermott said, "I have been horribly misquoted and people not cognizant of the true facts are censuring me right and left. The correspondents as well as some of the golfers at Shawnee took up my words in the wrong light and this caused all the trouble."

Little did the golf world know that Johnny had endured a heart-breaking experience that he was eating him up inside. He suffered heavy stock market losses that nearly wiped him out financially—mostly in highly speculative investments. Although he never revealed it publicly, it tormented him to lose the majority of his hard-earned money so quickly and needlessly.

Nevertheless, with high expectations of winning the U.S. Open for the third year in a row, Johnny came up short in 1913—finishing just four strokes out of first, but in eighth place, which was certainly a disappointment. However, McDermott helped coach Ouimet, who kept Johnny's promise that the foreign visitors wouldn't win the National Open that year. "Just play your own game," McDermott told Ouimet as he walked up to the first tee. "Pay no attention to Vardon and Ray."

About three weeks after his disappointing U.S. Open performance, however, McDermott managed to win the Western Open (in Memphis) to get back on top of the golf world again. After which, he headed down to Florida, where he worked as a golf instructor at the most exclusive hotels, sometimes earning as much as $100 a lesson—high fees in those days. His students happened to be among the famously wealthy, with names like Rockefeller, Vanderbilt and Astor. His Western Open win along with this cushy working vacation seemed to rejuvenate McDermott, returning him to a confident state of mind.

As the first major of 1914 rolled around—the British Open—Johnny entered it with hopes of climbing back on top in the golf world. He headed across the Atlantic to play in The Open at Prestwick, in Scotland. Due to travel blunders, he missed the ferry and train he needed to catch to get to the qualifying. Chagrined, he was forced to head home shortly after arrival.

Shipwrecked and worse

The only thing that could have made matters worse was if he wound up in a shipwreck—and that's what happened. Returning home on the Kaiser Wilhelm II, a grain carrier collided with the ship in the English Channel. McDermott and the rest of passengers had to float back to England in crowded lifeboats. McDermott eventually made it back to the states, but could never seem to shake the incident. While he seemed unharmed, the experience haunted him far more than anyone could have imagined.

The following month, Johnny played in the U.S. Open, but finished ninth. By that point, wrote James Finegan in *A Centennial Tribute to Golf in Philadelphia*, "The indomitable—some would say abrasive—self-confidence that had always marked his demeanor was nowhere in evidence." When a pro golfer loses his confidence, he's dead in the water. McDermott understood that only too well—not realizing it was still possible for him to turn his life, and golf game, around.

After his devastating financial losses, the British Open fiasco, the shipwreck, and believing he had lost his golf game, Johnny reached the point of giving up on life. The 1914 U.S. Open wound up being Johnny's final major. Later that year his parents checked him into a mental hospital. Things turned even worse for McDermott, and in 1916 his mother committed him to the State Hospital for the Insane in Norristown, Pennsylvania—where she was ordered to pay $1.75 a week "for support of said lunatic in said Hospital, until further notice." They labeled Johnny a lunatic!

Here's a young man who had won two U.S. Opens. Yet, it was if he had never amounted to anything, nor had any chance of recovering from his mental breakdown. It's incomprehensible how people could treat Johnny so despicably. The life of Johnny McDermott the golfer was over and he would never be more than a shell of the star he used to be. McDermott's fate reminds us that golf is a game demanding great mental strength and confidence. In his case, his whole existence revolved around golf. He didn't even have a girlfriend. He was married to golf. He had nothing to replace the void.

I'm convinced Johnny brainwashed himself into believing he had lost his game. His ninth-place finish in the U.S. Open demonstrated his talent was still there. In his second and third rounds, respectively, he tied Hagen (the winner), and beat him by a stroke.

His depression appeared to be mislabeled as insanity and, sadly, Johnny did not get the mental health care he needed. The remaining 55-plus years of McDermott's life had to have been a living hell. He deserves to be recognized for the young golf star he was.

Golf Magazine prints a mean portrayal

McDermott was a highly talented young man whom history has treated rather shabbily. My friend and author Bill Kelly and I were dismayed to read John Garitty's article, "The Curious Case of John McDermott," in the May 2, 2012, issue of *Golf Magazine* and find him described as a "famously rude, combative, abrasive, embarrassing, insane bigot, best left forgotten."

In 1997 Bill wrote *Birth of the Birdie—The First 100 Years of Golf at Atlantic City Country Club*, which I highly recommend to every golf historian. Chapter 10 gives a great account of McDermott's life story. Bill writes that the legend of Johnny McDermott espouses the spirit of a young America—the spunky, brash teenager who finally beat the Europeans at their own game. His name will never be eclipsed in the record book because he claimed many firsts—the first American, the first American to repeat, the first to break par and the youngest.

At the Atlantic City Country Club (ACCC) Johnny McDermott still has the reputation for being a young, brash and determined gentleman who didn't throw his clubs, drink or curse and attended mass every day before going to work, where he was highly regarded as the golf professional. I was particularly surprised to learn that he attended mass every day! He sounds more saintly than the terrible person *Golf Magazine* made him out to be. Bill Kelly and I thought we had researched the life of McDermott thoroughly but we both somehow missed the "bigot" and parts "best left forgotten."

McDermott had a typical Irish-American view of the British and Scot pros, who dominated the game in America and won the U.S. National Championship for its first 16 consecutive years until he came along. Maybe McDermott was a bit rude in calling Alex Smith a "big lout" after losing the 1910 Open in a playoff, but he was only 18 years old at the time, and he did make good on his promise to beat Smith the next time they met.

McDermott's "bigoted" view of the British of that era may have been justified. It was supported by Walter Travis, who won the U.S. Amateur at the ACCC before he won the British Amateur. He was so rudely treated by the British he refused to return to defend his title, especially after his center-shafted putter was retroactively banned by the Royal & Ancient Order of what he considered Snobs. *Asses* seems more appropriate—considering how they banned Travis's perfectly legal putter simply because they didn't want to see a working-class American win the British Open. This is despite the fact that most U.K. golfers who had previously won The Open (Vardon, Braid and Taylor included) grew up in poverty.

British snobbery

Walter Hagen, McDermott's friend and colleague, confirmed their view when he took exception to the British rule that golf pros were not permitted in the clubhouse dining room, and refused to play until the rules were changed. And John B. Kelly, another ACCC member and Olympic rowing champion, was banned from participating in the Henley regatta because he was a bricklayer and not considered a gentleman.

It wasn't McDermott who had bad manners and had to be taught a lesson, it was the U.K. professionals who thought they could win the U.S. Open trophy just by showing up, and it was McDermott—the young, brash and determined teenager who taught them a lesson. He did it again at Shawnee in 1913, shortly before the U.S Open at Brookline, when he handily won the preliminary tournament by eight strokes.

That's when McDermott gave his famous speech, promising to keep the U.S. Open trophy in America, which generated international interest in the game and took golf off the sports pages and onto the front pages of newspapers across the United States and the British Empire. That speech set the stage for the showdown at Brookline, coined "the Greatest Game" not because a local amateur won it, but because McDermott made it so. The international spirit inflamed by McDermott's "combative" style can still be felt today during Walker, Ryder and

Curtis Cup tournaments, and other "friendly competitions between nations," especially between the U.S.A. and Europe.

McDermott's seven professional tournament wins include the 1910 Philadelphia Open, the 1911 U.S. Open, the 1911 Philadelphia Open, the 1912 U.S. Open, the 1913 Philadelphia Open, the 1913 Western Open and the 1913 Shawnee Open.

"The Greatest Game" was a whiff

In the 2005 movie, "The Greatest Game Ever Played," I think "The Biggest Fraud Ever Filmed" would be a more appropriate title—in terms of its reckless portrayal of characters and events of the 1913 U.S. Open. Wilfred Reid was introduced as the British Amateur champion. However, Reid turned pro at in 1901, twelve years before the Open at Brookline. Not only was he not the Amateur champion, he was a seasoned professional. How was it possible for Bill Paxton, the film's director, to screw things up that badly??

Furthermore, in the movie, Reid gloats at the dinner table to Vardon and Ray about the superiority of sophisticated culture. After he disparages Jersey (where Vardon and Ray grew up), Ray nonchalantly punches Reid in the nose and knocks him over. Reid gets up with a bloodied nose and asks Vardon how he looks, to which Vardon replies disdainfully, "It's an improvement". Clearly, Vardon disliked Reid and wanted nothing to do with him. ALL OF THIS WAS WRONG!! Reid was not part of the upper class. He was a commoner like Vardon and Ray. Not only were Wilfred and Harry close friends. Reid was a protégé of Vardon and Harry helped him get a club professional job twelve years earlier when Reid was only 17.

It's true that Ray did take a swing at Reid, but he missed hitting him and his loss of temper had nothing to do with snobish comments from Reid. It had more to do with the fact that Ray had been drinking too much. They had gotten into a political discussion and Reed questioned how Ray could be a socialist when he was making so much money playing golf—which was a reasonable question. In the movie, Ray didn't feel the least bit of shame about his violent behavior or lack of concern for Reid's wellbeing. In reality, Ray was nothing like the uncouth bully that the movie made him out to be. Ted actually apologized later to Wilfred for taking a swing at him, even though he missed hitting him. Reed played in the Open the next day without a mark on his face—as opposed to the movie's depiction of him looking like he'd been in a brawl.

In regards to McDermott, It would have been hard for Paxton to cast an actor who looked any less like him than Michael Weaver. Weaver is a tall, stocky, reddish-haired man with a mustache and an unruly shock of hair. The real McDermott was short, thin, and clean-shaven with brown hair combed neatly across his forehead.

There's a scene in the movie portraying the second and final day of the 1913 U.S. Open, when McDermott has a mental meltdown. He nearly busts out of his suspenders as he swings, and his face is in a state of shock as his ball slices deep into the woods. Like a villain in some low-budget B movie, McDermott drops his club and collapses in horror, a broken man who would never finish the tournament.

But none of that ever happened! McDermott completed the 36-hole final day of regulation play, in extremely difficult cold, rainy weather, without incident. He turned in a respectable score of 308 (+12), an eighth-place finish and just four strokes out a tie for first. Granted, it must have been a disappointing finish for a young golf sensation who won The Open the previous two years in a row. However, his less-than-stellar play had a lot to do with the weather—which could be blamed on the fact that the tournament had been pushed back to late September to accommodate the famous Harry Vardon's availability to travel to America.

McDermott never had a mental breakdown of any kind during the 1913 U.S. Open. In fact, he went on to play in the British Open that year at Royal Liverpool and finish in a tie for fifth, the highest finish by an American to that date. His tragic mental illness didn't afflict McDermott until 1914 at age 22, yet Bill Paxton had the indecency to strike young Johnny with that cruel illness a year earlier than it actually happened. McDermott had to have been in pretty good shape mentally, at that time in his life, because three weeks later he won the Western Open.

Paxton also whiffed when he cast the actor to play Harry Vardon. In this stupid movie, Harry is a tall, sturdy, clean-shaven man. In real life, Vardon was of average height, a bit frail looking and wore a mustache. Paxton could have at least glanced at an old photo of Vardon to give himself some idea of what the man looked like.

I digress from Johnny McDermott, but a third strike against that movie is that Paxton attempts to change history and make the playoff far more dramatic than it actually was. In the movie, Ouimet won the playoff in a nail-biting finish, after barely coaxing in a 4-foot knee-knocker on the final hole for a one-stroke victory.

Ouimet actually waltzed away with the playoff, easily beating Vardon by five strokes in shooting a 72 (a great score, at the time) to Vardon's 77. Ted Ray, the third man in the playoff, finished with a 78. The fact that Ouimet handily beat Vardon, who was exhausted, by putting on a ball-striking exhibition, was an amazing true story that viewers of this lousy movie were cheated out of watching.

Another complaint I have against this film is that Ouimet was depicted as an unknown 20-year-old caddie. The fact is that a year before the 1913 U.S. Open, Quimet was already recognized as one of the top amateur golfers in Massachusetts. The movie made it seem as if Quimet hadn't played any golf for months, until about two weeks prior to the U.S. Open. In reality, two months prior to The Open, Ouimet not only played in the Massachusetts Amateur, he actually won the dang thing! How in the hell did something that significant get left out of this movie? His game had to have been quite sharp to win his state amateur. A month before The Open, Ouimet played in the U.S. Amateur and made it all the way to the quarterfinals, before being eliminated. Just before The Open, he teamed with McDermott in an 18-hole challenge match against Vardon and Ray in which the youngsters won. Why was nothing mentioned about that? The film's omissions and historical errors remind me of cringing while watching the scene in the movie "True Lies," when Bill Paxton wets his pants.

Finally, regarding this movie, a New England man by the name of Chuck Burgess informed me that his grandfather was the golf professional who taught Quimet—starting as a freshman in high school. Chuck managed to count 54 errors in the movie, not including casting, without doing any research. Of course, if they had removed the casting errors, there wouldn't have been a movie left to watch—which would have been a blessing.

Not to diminish Ouimet's U.S. Open win, but it's sad that he receives far more recognition for that single win than McDermott is given for his back-to-back Open titles at ages 19 and 20—not to mention his tie for first as an 18-year-old (before losing in a playoff), along with his five other professional wins between 18 and 21.

Along with Bill Kelly, I felt it my duty to correct *Golf Magazine's* mischaracterization of Johnny McDermott, and the way in which he was portrayed in Bill Paxton's cinematic attempt to rewrite U.S. Open history. The true story should be known of the great American teenage champion who sparked and inspired today's international competitions.

What's amazing to me is that Johnny managed to dominate the game as a teenager using a double-overlap grip, with only eight fingers touching the club. He was just a short, skinny kid who weighed about 135 pounds but could produce his wristy swing as hard and hit the ball as far as any of the top players, beating big, strong, experienced men at their own game.

In my eye, Johnny McDermott holds the title of Greatest Teenage Golfer in American History. I can't envision another American teenager coming within miles of challenging Johnny's U.S. Open record, a tie for second and a win, not to mention his two teenage wins in the Philadelphia Open against a field of top professionals. Even Tiger Woods as a teenager never challenged McDermott's accomplishments.

Calls for action against *Golf Magazine* and Bill Paxton's "Greatest Game" film

In light of the golfing legend McDermott was, I urge all readers to send an email to *Golf Magazine*, demanding a retraction of their mischaracterization of Johnny McDermott in their May 2, 2012, issue. The article's comments amount to a vicious attack on a very nice young man who was golf's first American hero. Johnny deserves his fair credit and to not be forgotten!

Perhaps we should forget about *Golf Magazine* and not bother renewing our subscription to a publication that recklessly trashes one of our early American heroes! Please join me in demanding this retraction, with threat of boycott, should they ignore our demand. See my letter of demand to *Golf Magazine* in the appendix.

Additionally, Bill Paxton needs to give a long-overdue public apology for his erroneous portrayal of McDermott in "The Greatest Game."

CHAPTER 6

TOMMY ARMOUR

The Silver Scot

Thomas Dickson Armour was born in Edinburgh, Scotland on September 24, 1894 and died in Larchmont, New York on Spttember 11, 1968. He was the son of George Armour, a confectioner. His mother's name is unknown. His father died when Armour was four. Armour's older brother, Sandy, took the young child to a golf course adjacent to their house and introduced him to the game of golf. As an adolescent, Armour caddied for Sandy as he won the Scottish Amateur championship. After entering Stewart's College in Edinburgh, Armour graduated from the University of Edinburgh in 1914.

Although Armour was considered a promising young amateur golfer in Scotland during his years at the university, he enlisted in the Black Watch Regiment in the latter part of 1914, thus thrusting him into World War I. During the war Armour established a reputation as being one of the fastest and deadliest machine gunners in his entire regiment.

During his service in World War 1 he rose from private to staff major in the Tank Corps. His conduct earned him a special meeting with King George V. In

1918 Armour transferred to the newly established Tank Corps; in June of that year his tank was shelled by enemy fire, and he was one of only two survivors. Tragically, before the end of the war Armour fell victim to a mustard gas attack, resulting in a heavily wounded left arm and temporary blindness in both eyes. Although the arm would eventually heal (yet remain in a weakened condition), he permanently lost sight in his left eye.

In 1920, the year after his marriage to Consuelo Carrera (the couple would have two children), Armour won the French Amateur before sailing to the U.S. with his family and meeting Walter Hagen. Through Walter's help, Tommy was hired as secretary of the Westchester-Biltmore Club. Soon after, he received U.S. citizenship and began competing in amateur tournaments in the next four years. In 1921 Armour competed in an international amateur golf competition between Great Britain and the United States. This event, which Armour helped win for Great Britain, would be recognized as the precursor to the inauguration of the biannual Walker Cup matches one year later. Of course, the year this event became really huge was when Walker, Texas Ranger, started backing it.

In 1922 Armour became a citizen of the United States. Then in 1924, he turned pro, started giving lessons and competed in all the important professional events. The following year, he joined the American professional golf tour. Armour also accepted a position as club professional at the prestigious Congressional Country Club in Washington, D.C., in 1926 after briefly serving as secretary at the Westchester-Biltmore Country Club.

Although the "Silver Scot," so nicknamed for his hair color, had one victory on the professional tour in 1925, few expected the incredible success Armour enjoyed in 1927. He broke the single season record for tour victories, including one in the highly competitive Canadian Open. However, Armour's greatest victory that year occurred at the Oakmont Country Club in Pennsylvania, as he captured the U.S. Open. Armour, who throughout his career had a penchant for making seemingly impossible comebacks, birdied the final hole of regulation play to tie Harry Cooper with a score of 301, after holing a one-iron shot from the fairway; the following day Armour defeated Cooper by three strokes on the way to his first major championship. Later that year Armour participated in the first official Ryder Cup match, held at Worcester Country Club in Massachusetts and won convincingly by the American team.

Armour's life could best be described as a roller-coaster ride during the next few years. In 1928 he dominated the pro tour by winning four more tournaments. Yet in 1930 Armour underwent a highly publicized divorce from his wife, which was settled in April. Armour, who had fallen in love with Estelle Andrews, suffered substantial financial damages in the proceedings. (Armour and Andrews later married, and they would have one son.) However, later that year Armour entered the PGA Championhip at Fresh Meadow in Flushing, New York. Armour lost five of the first six holes against Johnny Farrell in the quarterfinal, but came back to win, 2 and 1. His opponent in the final was Sarazen, who was playing on his home course. All square going to the 36th hole, a par by Armour was good enough for a win over Sarazen, securing the PGA Championship title.

In 1931 Armour composed another improbable comeback, making up a five-stroke deficit in the final round and defeating Argentine Jose Jurado by one stroke to win the last of his major championships, the British Open at Carnoustie, Scotland. This early 1930s success of Armour's in the majors was overshadowed by Bobby Jones's Grand Slam, and Armour seems to have been overlooked.

Although Armour remained highly competitive on the professional tour for another five years, at this point in his life he established himself as one of the most respected (and highly priced) golf instructors in the world. Armour held the position of golf instructor at the Boca Raton Club in Florida for almost twenty-five years, teaching and correcting the swings of noted golfers such as Babe Didrikson Zaharias and Lawson Little. In 1940 he was elected to the PGA Hall of Fame. In the 1950s Armour frequented Winged Foot Country Club in Mamaroneck, New York, while authoring instruction manuals and arguing for the importance of a dominant right hand throughout the swing. He also designed golf clubs for the Crawford, McGregor and Canby Company. Armour died in Larchmont, New York.

While his professional career was relatively short, the legacy Armour left on the game of golf will never be forgotten. He was not considered to be the nicest guy on the tour, he was deeply admired for his unyielding determination to win (or in the case of battle, to survive and recover). He was a highly sought after golf instructor, and his books have remained relevant. Armour will always be remembered for his uncanny ability to bounce back. In the process Armour changed the game of golf and molded generations of successful players.

Who coined the term "yips"? Tommy Armour

Armour was a great golfer who could have become one of the top 10 greatest, had he not been cursed by the yips during the prime of his career. Armour is credited with creating the term for this mental golf disorder, which robbed him of making short putts on a regular basis, starting in 1927. He said of the yips, "Once you've got 'em, you've got 'em."

Yet he won two majors after his game was unglued by the yips at the Shawnee Open in 1927, in which he scored a 23 on the par-5 17th hole. That is a record high single-hole score in professional competition that has never been beat. Assuming he reached the green in regulation (or thereabouts), he must have taken somewhere in the neighborhood of 20 putts on that one hole. His hands must have been shaking like a leaf. That's what I call a horrific case of the yips!

Armour co-wrote the book *How to Play Your Best Golf All the Time* (1953) with Herb Graffis. For many years it was the best-selling golf book ever. A series of 8mm films based on the book was released by Castle Films, including "Short Game" (parts I and II), "Long Hitting Clubs," "Grip" and "Stance."

Armour was inducted into the World Golf Hall of Fame in 1976. He died in Larchmont, New York, Sept. 11, 1968, two weeks shy of his 74th birthday. He was cremated at the Fern Cliff Cemetery in Hartsdale, New York. The Tommy Armour irons became a top set in the 1980s and 1990s, and were used by numerous touring pros and top amateurs. To this day, metal woods, irons, golf balls and travel carriers are still marketed in the Armour name.

Quotes by and about Tommy Armour

"Golf is an awkward set of bodily contortions designed to produce a graceful result."

"Just knock the hell out of it with your right hand."

"The most abysmal advice ever given is by the ignorant to the stupid."

"It is not solely the capacity to make great shots that makes champions, but the essential quality of making very few bad shots."

Author Ross Goodner: *"At one time or another, he was known as the greatest iron player, the greatest raconteur, the greatest drinker and the greatest and most expensive teacher in golf. Nothing was ever small about Tommy Armour's reputation."*

Bernard Darwin *was most impressed with Armour's ability to strike a golf ball.* "I do not believe that (J.H.) Taylor or (Harry) Vardon at their best ever gave themselves so many possible putts for three with their iron shots as he does," *Darwin once wrote.* "His style is the perfection of rhythm and beauty."

Herbert Warren Wind: *"Whenever the Silver Scot played himself into a contending position, he always seemed to have that extra something that was the difference between barely losing and barely winning. He was singularly unaffected by the pressure of the last stretch. His hands were hot but his head was cool."*

Lawson Little: *Tommy Armour was responsible for all of the success I had in golf.*

The great golf writer, **Charles Price**, *described Armour as having* "a dash of indifference, a touch of class, (and) a bit of majesty."

Julius Boros: *Tommy Armour was a genius at teaching you how to play your best golf.*

Bobby Cruickshank, *claiming to know Armour for 60 years, said,* "He was the kindest, best-hearted fellow you ever saw."

Jeff Gold: *"Tommy Armour was a complex man and misunderstood, but he seemed to like it that way."*

Here we have a pro golfer, coming from America and winning The Open Championship at a course near his birthplace in Edinburgh, Scottland. Armour won the 1931 British Open, his third and final major Championship, shooting 71 in the final round. This victory was considered Armour's finest moment. He won 25 PGA Tour events, including three majors, with a weakened left arm, vision in only one eye and the yips!

Tommy Armour major championship wins: three
1920   U.S. Open
1930   PGA Championship
1931   British Open

PGA Tour wins: 25
1920   Pinehurst Fall Pro-Am Bestball (as an amateur, with Leo Diegel)
1925   Florida West Coast Open

1926 Winter Pro Golf Championship

1927 Long Beach Open, El Paso Open, U.S. Open, Canadian Open, Oregon Open

1928 Metropolitan Open, Philadelphia Open Championship, Pennsylvania Open Championship, Sacramento Open

1929 Western Open

1930 Canadian Open, PGA Championship, St. Louis Open

1931 The Open Championship

1932 Miami International Four-Ball (with Ed Dudley), Mid-South Bestball (with Al Watrous), Miami Open

1934 Canadian Open, Pinehurst Fall Pro-Pro (with Bobby Cruickshank)

1935 Miami Open

1936 Walter Olson Golf Tournament (tie with Willie Macfarlane)

1938 Mid-South Open

Other wins

1920 French Amateur

1927 Miami International Four-Ball (with Bobby Cruickshank)

1938 Mid-South Pro/Pro (with Bobby Cruickshank; tie with Henry Picard and Jack Grout)

CHAPTER 7

BOBBY LOCKE

Blackballed by the PGA Tour

W as this a shameful period in the history of the PGA Tour? Or did Locke deserve what he got? You be the judge. **Arthur "Bobby" Locke**, who lived from Nov. 20, 1917, to March 9, 1987, changed his first name to Bobby in deference to the golf-world hero of his time, Bobby Jones—a little known fact overlooked by most golf historians.

This forgotten golf legend was the first South African to achieve success internationally. He won four Open Championships between 1949 and 1957 in a career that included 72 professional wins. Ten were PGA Tour events while playing in the U.S. from 1947 to 1949. South African golf legend Gary Player describes him as the greatest putter of all time.

Locke was born in Germiston, South Africa. He won the South African Open as an amateur in 1935 at just age 17. Bobby would go on to win the event nine times. He played in his first Open Championship in 1936, when he was 18, and tied for eighth. He turned professional at 20 and became a dominant force in his native country, racking up a total of 38 wins on the South Africa Tour. His golf career was interrupted in World War II, by his military service from 1943 to 1945, in the South African Air Force.

By 1946, Locke's golf career was back in full swing. Late that year, he hosted American pro Sam Snead for a series of challenge matches in South Africa. It was a winner-take-all competition with $15,000 up for grabs. Locke put Snead to shame, winning 12 out of the 16 matches—pocketing the 15 grand like candy from a baby. Snead then made the mistake of inviting Locke to come to the U.S. and give the PGA Tour a try. Locke was quick to accept.

Locke arrived in the U.S. for the first time in April 1947, four months into the PGA Tour. Despite a late start, Locke dominated the PGA Tour, winning six tournaments (including four in a five-week period), and finishing second to Jimmy Demaret on the Money List. By the end of the 1949 PGA Tour season, Locke had played in 59 events in which he won 11, and finished in the top three in 30, more than half the events. You can bet that many of Snead's PGA Tour brethren were fuming over Snead's inviting a "ringer"—as Locke turned out—to join their tour.

As time went on, things only become more contemptuous. They started taunting Locke, calling him Old Muffin Face—yet it was rather fitting, in light of his large, round face that rarely changed expression.

Locke delivered a staggering performance in the 1948 Chicago Victory National that proved to be the last straw, as far as PGA Tour members were concerned. He won that tournament by 16 strokes and made a mockery out of the field. By this time it became obvious that this ridiculously talented, pudgy South African golfer had overstayed his welcome and it was time for him to leave.

In 1949, Locke was officially banned from the PGA Tour, after winning his first Open Championship that year, and he remained in Great Britain to play in a series of exhibitions and autumn events. My guess is Locke set himself up to be banned. He made it easy for the tour to do, as he had failed, without explanation, to appear at several PGA Tour events to which he had committed. The unsuppressed animosity toward Locke escalated on the PGA Tour to the point which it was more than he could stand. Thus, he decided to bow out without incident and go back to playing on tours that welcomed him.

Locke's ban was lifted in 1951, but, except for rare appearances, he chose not to return to the United States. Bobby Locke is only one of two golfers who were, essentially, blackballed from playing on the PGA Tour for being too good. (Read about the other one in Chapter 13.)

Being the only golfer on tour who wore the nostalgic knickers, white shoes, and stockings—copying Bobby Jones's style of that bygone era—caused Locke to stick out like a sore thumb.

Further irritating his playing partners, Locke was notorious for being a slow player. Here's what the World Golf Hall of Fame says about Locke's slow play, "On the golf course, he moved at a maddeningly slow pace. Large gaps would open in front of him, his playing partners would grow red-necked in anger, officials would threaten penalties, but Locke was unyielding. He never lost his temper or expressed annoyance and was described as cool, shrewd and imperturbable."

Despite his detractors, Locke built his success on his incredible putting ability. Have you ever heard the expression, "You drive for show, but putt for dough?" Locke reportedly coined it. It was Locke's putting that really set him apart from other pros of his time. Watching a video of Locke's putting is almost painful. His putting stroke, undoubtedly, really drove his opponents crazy. Seeing him putt, (with his ancient, beat up wooden shafted putter) I wondered how this guy could even excel at amateur golf, much less at the professional level.

I've always attempted a pendulum putting stroke, keeping the putter going straight back and through. Bobby Locke's stroke was the opposite. He had a pronounced hooking action in his putting stroke, in which he would take his putter back way inside, and rotate his wrists to the left on the follow through. To putt consistently well, he had to reproduce that same hooking action every stroke—along with having his ball position exactly the same every time. It also required him to play for extra break to the left, to allow for the hook spin. He was well known as a putting genius and having a great eye for reading breaks.

It's been said by Gary Player, and others who played frequently with him, that every time Bobby played, he put on a veritable putting clinic. Player boldly commented that because of his superior putting ability, Locke could beat Ben Hogan and Snead like a drum when they were in their prime. That may have been true when Locke's putting was particularly sharp. However, if Hogan had been able to putt like Locke, he may have won every tournament he entered from 1940 to 1960—as Player would agree. Player also said that in the 100-plus rounds he played with Locke, he never saw him three-putt a single green. That sounds unbelievable, but it's beyond me to question the great Gary Player.

Locke was not long off the tee, but was a consistent ball striker, hitting a lot of fairways and greens with a strong draw on every full shot that resembled a hook—as opposed to Hogan who was nauseated by a hook and strongly preferred to play a fade.

After leaving the PGA Tour, Locke continued his career in Europe and Africa, where he felt more welcome—no one was trying to blackball him. He won 23 times in Europe. Most notable were his four wins in The Open Championship, which came in 1949, 1950, 1952 and 1957. His three wins in four years was amazing, but his win in the 1957 Open Championship was marred by controversy.

Locke had failed to properly replace his ball after marking on the 72nd green, and proceeded to putt out. This was confirmed by newsreel footage provided to the R&A after the trophy presentation. I haven't seen the video, but I'm guessing that he moved his mark out of his playing partner's line and forgot to replace it. The rules at the time made no provision for a two-shot penalty, thus Locke's win could have been overturned by disqualification. However, the championship committee did not enforce the disqualification rule, citing "equity and spirit of the game" as overriding factors to sustain the posted result. It would have been rather awkward for the committee to reverse its decision after declaring Locke the winner.

I'm glad the British Open Championship committee had more empathy and guts than the USGA would have. Undoubtedly, if that had been the U.S. Open, Locke would have been disqualified for that minor oversight that gave him no advantage over the rest of the field. Hopefully, in coming years, the USGA will advance its ruling decisions to where the British Open committee was back in 1957. Obviously, the USGA committee is comprised of very slow learners!

After leaving the PGA Tour, Locke played in many other parts of the world. Ironically, though, Bobby captured his very last tournament win in the 1959 New Hampshire Open—here in the U.S.A. where he had been blackballed 10 years before. You could say Locke had the last laugh.

A train crash, final torturous years and legacy in ruins

In 1960, Locke's car was struck by a train on the day of his daughter's birth! Bobby subsequently suffered from migraines and eye problems that put an end to his golf career at age 43.

Locke was elected to the World Golf Hall of Fame in 1977. He was only the second member after Gary Player who did not come from the United States or the United Kingdom.

Bobby's troubles continued after his playing days, most notably in 1979, when he shot and killed an unarmed man who demanded money that Locke owed him. Locke was given a 60- day suspended prison sentence for manslaughter. You probably don't want to hear, nor would Gary Player want me to tell you, that Locke murdered a poor black laborer by shooting him in the back. And that it was whitewashed and called merely manslaughter. After which, he avoided prison time and any probation requirements by merely paying a fine, in South African rand, that was equivalent to less than $140.

Sadly, Locke died at 69, after a brief illness, reportedly in a state of poverty. Nevertheless, Locke was a great golfer but forgotten, thanks to his shun from the PGA Tour. Never before or since has a foreign golfer strolled into this country and created such a firestorm by his domination over the U.S. top PGA Tour players. Adding insult was the fact that an overweight and out-of-shape South African was beating U.S. players with an unconventional playing style which no one in this country had ever seen. It was downright embarrassing.

In a crushing 1947 campaign, winning six PGA Tour events, after arriving mid-season, he won the 1948 Chicago Victory National by a whopping 16 strokes. It was terribly humiliating to PGA Tour players and they made it clear they wanted him out. Thus, Bobby's brilliant play in the U.S. was cut short and the PGA Tour did its best to sweep it under the rug.

In today's era of so many talented golfers from all over the world, we'll never see another foreign golfer in the U.S. so quickly become a golfing force. While Locke's reputation off the golf course is indefensible, I hope to restore his legacy in the U.S. and give him the recognition he is due for his highly unorthodox playing style, ruling golf in America so thoroughly, yet so briefly.

On the other hand, Bobby suffered a train wreck to both his person and reputation after committing a cold-blooded murder that was hush-hushed until now—by blowing the dust off that awful crime so the golf world learns the whole truth about Bobby Locke.

Bobby Locke professional wins: 72
Open Championship wins: four
PGA Tour wins: 15

1947	Canadian Open, Houston Open, Philadelphia Inquirer Open, All American Open, Columbus Open, Goodall Round Robin
1948	Phoenix Open, Chicago Victory Open
1949	Cavalier Invitational, Goodall Round Robin, **The Open Championship**
1950	All American Open, **The Open Championship**
1952	**The Open Championship**
1957	**The Open Championship**

Other wins: 57

1935	South African Open, Natal Open (both as amateur)
1936	Natal Open (amateur)
1937	South African Open (amateur)
1938	South African Open, Irish Open, New Zealand Open, South Africa Professional, Transvaal Open
1939	South African Open, Dutch Open, South Africa Professional, Transvaal Open
1940	South African Open, Transvaal Open, South Africa Professional
1946	South African Open, South Africa Professional, Transvaal Open, Yorkshire Evening News, British Masters, Brand Lochryn Tournament
1947	Carolinas Open, Carolinas PGA Championship
1948	Carolinas Open
1949	Transvaal Open
1950	South African Open, South Africa Professional, Transvaal Open, Dunlop Tournament, Spalding Tournament, North British Tournament
1951	South African Open, Transvaal Open, South Africa Professional
1952	French Open, Mexican Open, Lotus Tournament, Carolinas Open

1953 French Open, Natal Open

1954 Egyptian Open, German Open, Swiss Open, Dunlop Tournament, British Masters, Egyptian Match Play, Transvaal Open, Swallow-Harrogate Tournament

1955 Australian Open, Transvaal Open, South African Open, South Africa Professional

1957 Daks Tournament, Bowmaker Amateur-Professional

1958 Transvaal Open

1959 New Hampshire Open

CHAPTER 8

CARY MIDDLECOFF

*Perhaps best forgotten
or is that a bit harsh?*

I n terms of his slow play, perhaps it's for the best that this golf legend has become forgotten—considering how the World Golf Hall of Fame described his play as "glacially slow." On the other hand, Cary Middlecoff fans (the two who are still alive) may think differently.

The great thing about Middlecoff is that unlike Locke he never murdered anyone—assuming you don't count the people who may have died of old age waiting for him to hit his next shot.

Emmett Cary "Doc" Middlecoff was a dentist who gave up his practice to become a pro golfer on the PGA Tour in the 1940s—and it was a damn good thing he did. Middlecoff was born Jan. 6, 1921, in the one-horse town of Halls, Tennessee. (I understand that the town has since grown to two horses.) He played college golf at the University of Mississippi where he was the school's first All-American Golfer in 1939.Cary won the Tennessee State Amateur four straight years from 1940 to 1943, starting at age 19 and blew away the field in one collegiate tournament by 29 strokes.

After earning his doctor of dental surgery degree in 1944, he entered the U.S. Army Dental Corps during World War II and, briefly, practiced dentistry on military personnel. Actually, Middlecoff came very close to giving up golf for dentistry before serving 18 months and working on over 7,000 sets of teeth. That experience gave him an appreciation of how much more enjoyable it would be to play golf for a living as opposed to drilling teeth. Then after he made this change in career choice, it was like pulling teeth to get him off the golf course.

Cary became the first amateur to win the North and South Open, in 1945, while playing in the final group with Ben Hogan and Gene Sarazen. That victory, undoubtedly, convinced him that he could compete successfully on the PGA Tour. However, he waited until 1947 to turn pro and won the Charlotte open that year, while tying the course record in the final round—taking home a whopping check of $2,000. This was validation that he made the right decision in turning pro. However, beating Hogan and Sarazen, two years prior, would have been enough validation for me. Why wait two more years?

During his playing career from 1945 to 1961, Middlecoff won 40 PGA Tour events, including the 1955 Masters and two U.S. Open wins in 1949 and 1956. Cary is only one of nine golfers in history to win 40 tournaments or more on the PGA Tour (counting his two wins in Four-Ball competition). Middlecoff led the tour in wins three times, with seven titles in 1949, six in 1951 and six in 1955. In 1956, he won the Vardon Trophy for lowest-scoring average. He played on three Ryder Cup teams: 1953, 1955 and 1959.

Middlecoff's most dominant career performance came in the 1955 Masters, which he won by a then-record seven strokes, ignited by holing a 90-foot eagle putt on the 13th during the third round. When he held off Ben Hogan and Julius Boros at the 1946 U.S. Open, played at Oak Hill, Middlecoff established himself as one of the most dominent golfers of the 1950s.

During the 1950s, Cary won 28 titles, more than any other golfer in that decade. He was tall, at 6 feet 2 inches, and was renowned for having tremendous length off the tee and the ability to overpower golf courses as well as his opponents. His length, along with good accuracy made him a formidable opponent. During his best year, he was also considered a great putter. And he was known for taking excessive time to play his shots. Back problems brought on by his exaggerated reverse C finish and crouched-putting method, in addition to struggles with the deadly yips, brought an end to his career in the early 1960s while he was only in his early 40s.

In 1986, Middlecoff was inducted into the World Golf Hall of Fame. He died of heart disease Sept. 1, 1998, at 77, in Memphis, Tennessee.

Among Cary' more memorable phrases were, "Nobody wins the Open. It wins you," and "Anyone who hasn't been nervous, or hasn't choked somewhere down the line, is an idiot."

Slowest great golfer to ever play the game

There's no question that Cary Middlecoff was a great golfer. Although he never took a lesson, he had a swing that Bobby Jones envied. "I'd give the world to have a swing like that," Jones once commented. Middlecoff won 36 tournaments on the PGA Tour, plus three majors (two U.S. Opens and a Masters). Doc had six-win seasons in 1949, 1951 and 1955. It's impressive that Middlecoff was able to play so well without a lesson or swing coach.

However, history knocks Middlecoff by making his slow play more legendary than his playing ability. He was so unbearably slow that he made Glen Day's pace of play look half way decent—if that's possible. (They don't nickname a golfer "All Day" for nothing.)

In the 36-hole final of the 1955 PGA, Middlecoff was playing against Doug Ford and lit a cigarette when he arrived at the green on one hole. Did Doc drop his cigarette on the ground, when it came his turn to putt, like every smoker I've ever played with? Hell, no. Before putting, he stood there and smoked the cigarette until it was gone! Reportedly, the gallery gave him a hard time about the incident. For crying out loud, I would hope they did! But according to Ford, "You couldn't rush Doc and I didn't care." The reason Ford didn't care is because he waited comfortably sitting in the chair his son had shrewdly brought along. This worked out well for Ford. He won the match fairly easily, by a four and three margin.

At the 1957 U.S. Open, defending champion Middlecoff closed with a pair of 68s at Inverness, coming from behind and forcing an 18-hole playoff with Dick Meyer. Dick learned from Ford's son, and brought a camping stool to the playoff—apparently waiting for Middlecoff to play a shot was akin to a camp-out. Again, the chair-sitting seemed to rattle Doc because he played like crap, shooting a 79. Meyer shot 72 and coasted to an easy victory while Middlecoff missed his opportunity to be one of very few golfers to win back-to-back U.S. Opens.

Golf writer Dan Jenkins was the first person to correctly identify the reason why Middlecoff had to quit dentistry—it was because no one could hold their mouth open that long. The funny thing is that some people actually thought Jenkins was joking.

Stories have been told about how Middlecoff was even known to stop at the top of his backswing and just wait there for a while. Middlecoff had to have been golf's slowest great player. It's inconceivable that any successful pro golfer would get by playing as slow as Cary Middlecoff—especially now that the PGA Tour is cracking down on slow play by putting slow groups on time clocks and assessing penalties to chronically slow players. Nevertheless, in the '40s and '50s, Middlecoff managed to carve out a pretty remarkable career, despite making Glen Day look (let's just say) not terribly slow.

What seems odd to me is that along with being a slow, methodical player, the WGHOF described Middlecoff as having a volcanic temper. Those traits usually don't go together. Apparently, after Cary was born, they broke the mold—perhaps for the good.

In the case of this forgotten golfing legend, if *Golf Magazine* had said he is best left forgotten, I would have agreed—in terms of his slow play. On the other hand, Cary Middlecoff was a tremendously talented, self-taught golfer and one of the best of his time. No one can take that away from him. One might comment that Middlecoff got away with murder by that cigarette stunt he pulled in the 1955 PGA—smoking the entire cancer stick before hitting his putt. Compared to Bobby Locke, however, Cary was an angel.

Cary Middlecoff professional wins: 40
Major championship wins: three
1949   U.S. Open
1955   Masters
1956   U.S. Open

PGA Tour wins: 38

1945   North and South Open (as an amateur)

1947   Charlotte Open

1948   Hawaiian Open

1949   Rio Grande Valley Open, Jacksonville Open, U.S. Open, Motor City Open (co-winner with Lloyd Mangrum), Reading Open

1950   Houston Open, Jacksonville Open, St. Louis Open

1951   Lakewood Park Open, Colonial National Invitation, All American Open, Eastern Open, St. Louis Open, Kansas City Open

1952   El Paso Open, Motor City Open, St. Paul Open, Kansas City Open

1953   Houston Open, Palm Beach Round Robin, Carling Open

1954   Motor City Open

1955   Bing Crosby Pro-Am Invitational, St. Petersburg Open, Masters Tournament, Western Open, Miller High Life Open, Cavalcade of Golf

1956   Bing Crosby National Pro-Am Golf Championship, Phoenix Open, U.S. Open

1958   Miller Open Invitational

1959   St. Petersburg Open Invitational

1961   Memphis Open Invitational

Ryder Cup

1953, 1955, 1959 (winners)

Other wins

1948   Miami International Four-Ball (with Jim Ferrier)

1949   Greenbrier Pro-Am, Miami International Four-Ball (with Jim Ferrier)

CHAPTER 9

PETER THOMSON

Greatest Aussie golfer

Peter William Thomson, born Aug. 23, 1929, at 85 as of this writing is an Australian most famous for his five wins in The Open Championship. This golf legend won 70 professional tournaments worldwide, prior to joining the U.S. Senior Tour in 1984. After turning 50, he went on to win 11 Senior Tour events in a two-year period, including one major—the 1984 PGA Seniors Championship, giving him a total of six career major.

As a boy, he would sneak on to a nine-hole course named Royal Park. When the members saw his talent, he was given free playing privileges, and by age 15 was the club champion. After a two-year apprenticeship as an assistant pro along Melbourne's famed sandbelt, Thomson turned pro and quickly dominated Australian golf. "I sensed he had that inevitable something when I first set eyes on him," said the great Australian pro, Norman von Nida. As a young professional, he was profoundly influenced by Bobby Locke, Ben Hogan and Sam Snead.

Peter was gifted with the ability to relish and play his very best under the intense pressure of the closing holes of a championship. In his biography he wrote, "That was the real thrill of it for me. I've seen a lot of people find themselves in that situation, and I suspect that very few of them like it, but I really enjoyed it." He once wrote, "The most important facets of golf are careful planning, calm and clear thinking and the ordinary logic of common sense."

The World Golf Hall of Fame describes Thomson as a thinking man's golfer with a clean, brisk game which was based on cold logic and a gift for reducing things to their simplest essentials. His style was free of the extraneous, so that the path he would take to victory seemed a remarkably straight line.

He dominated the Senior Tour in 1985, reeling off nine tournament wins in that year alone. What's shocking is he never won another Senior Tour event. Peter underscores the thinking, at the time, that senior golfers hit a brick wall after age 55—as Thomson apparently did at the end of 1985, upon turning 56.

Still Thomson is the greatest Australian golfer of all time. Greg Norman is often thought of as the greatest Australian golfer, having spent 331 weeks as the world's No. 1 and chalking up a total of 89 professional wins, including 20 PGA Tour wins. However, if there's a high premium on major championship wins, as I believe there should, Thomson has Norman beat, hands down, with a total of six majors to Norman's two.

Additionally, Thomson played in a mere 12 U.S. majors during his regular career. This compares to Norman's entering 65 U.S. majors with no wins. The bottom line is Thomson won three times as many majors as Norman, despite playing in far fewer of them. Anyone who says Norman is the greatest Australian golfer doesn't know what they're talking about.

I recently asked a 20-something golfer what the name Peter Thomson meant to him. "Do you mean Peter Frampton?" he replied. That was harsh. He remembered the name of a washed- up '70s rock star, but not the greatest Australian golfer of all time!

Forget Greg Norman

Young golfers of America: Forget about Greg Norman. He tended to be a choker in the tournaments that mattered most. But not Peter Thompson. Among his six major wins, he won three Open Championships in a row. A pro golfer who has any tendency to choke under pressure like Norman could never dream of accomplishing that feat. Going back as far as 1950, Peter is the only golfer in the world to win the same major three years in a row.

It's unlikely that will be matched again by any golfer. Greg Norman never successfully defended any of his official tournament wins on either the PGA or European Tour. I still think Greg was a great golfer and a good guy. I have to give him a hard time, though, for throwing away so many majors. If Norman had been as unflappable as Billy Casper (see Chapter 10) he might have won many more.

It's mind-boggling that a guy with Norman's talent could end his career with zero major wins in the U.S. after 65 tries. Norman's 1996 Masters meltdown has to go down as the worst final-day choke by a tournament leader in major championship history. I wouldn't have thought it possible for a pro golfer to start the final round with a six-stroke lead and lose it by five.

Yet it's hard to not feel for a guy who wears his agony on his shirt sleeve. Greg gained twice as many die-hard fans that day, by choking his guts out, than he would have if he had won the one tournament that meant more to him than anything.

Thomson rarely played in the U.S. but he won often in his native Australia, and Europe and Asia during his prime in the 1950s. His Open Championship wins came in 1954, 1955, 1956, 1958 and 1965. He was the only man to win the tournament for three consecutive years in the 20th century. Equally impressive, during one seven-year stretch from 1952 to 1958, Thomson finished no worse than *second* in the British Open. He won the first and last of his Open titles at Royal Birkdale.

Peter was a prolific tournament champion around the world, winning the national championships of 10 countries, including the New Zealand Open nine times. He competed in the PGA Tour in 1953 and 1954 with relatively little success, finishing 44th and 25th on the Money List, and after that was an infrequent competitor. However in 1956, playing in just eight events, he won the rich Texas International with a huge first prize of $13,478. He accomplished that win in a three-way playoff over Cary Middlecoff (of all people) and Gene Litler, after shooting blazing final round of 63. That year he achieved his best finish in one of the U.S. majors, fourth at the U.S. Open, to finish ninth on the Money List.

In the era when Thomson won his first four Open Championships, very few top American golfers traveled to the U.K. to play in that event. At that time, the prize money in The Open was so low that the winner's share wasn't enough to cover their travel and lodging expenses. However, in his 1965 victory, Thomson proved he was capable of beating the PGA Tour's very best players. This was against a field that included Jack Nicklaus, Arnold Palmer and Tony Lema. Those three were ranked 1, 2 and 4, respectively, on the 1964 Money List. Only Billy Caper, No. 3, was missing. Thomson beat defending champion Lema by four strokes, with Nicklaus and Palmer finishing a distant nine and 10 strokes behind, respectively.

Thomson's last tournament victory was in the 1988 British PGA Seniors Championship, the year he was inducted into the World Golf Hall of Fame. He was president of the Australian PGA from 1962 to 1964, and the victorious non-playing captain of the International Team in the 1998 President's Cup.

Thomson's third consecutive Open Championship

Peter Thomson won his third consecutive Open Championship in 1956 at Royal Liverpool by three strokes over the famous Flory Van Donck of Belgium. The winner's share was 1,000 pounds. What in the world did Peter do with all that money? I hope he gave some to charity.

Fifty-eight years ago, Peter Thomson became the last golfer to win the same major three years in a row. I predict Peter will go down in history as the last golfer to ever "three-pete" in a major. In today's age of ever-increasing competition, it has become impossible for any future golfer to duplicate. Peter should be remembered as the last "three-peter."

The other spelling of this hyphenated word is trademarked by former basketball coach Pat Riley. However, I must say that "Peter the three-peter" has a great ring to it—thus, I decree Peter Thomson shall be known as such. It's high time he receives the accolades he deserves for that amazing accomplishment in 1956—never to be repeated.

Peter Thomson professional wins: 82
Open Championship wins: five
PGA Tour wins: six
1954   The Open Championship
1955   The Open Championship
1956   Texas International Open, **The Open Championship**
1958   The Open Championship
1965   The Open Championship

The Open Championship was not sanctioned by the PGA Tour in Thomson's era, but pre-1995 British Open wins were retroactively classified as PGA Tour wins in 2002.

Australian Tour wins: 34

1947   Australian Foursomes Shield (with H.R. Payne)
1948   Victoria Amateur Championship
1950   New Zealand Open
1951   Australian Open, New Zealand Open
1952   Victorian PGA Championship, Mobilco Tournament
1953   New Zealand Open, New Zealand PGA Championship, Victorian PGA Championship, Ampol Tournament
1955   New Zealand Open, Pelaco Tournament, Speedo Tournament
1956   Pelaco Tournament
1958   Victorian Open, Pelaco Tournament
1959   New Zealand Open, Pelaco Tournament, Cole 3,000 Tournament
1960   New Zealand Open, Wills Masters
1961   New Zealand Open, Adelaide Advertiser, New South Wales Open
1965   New Zealand Open
1967   New Zealand Caltex Tournament, Australian PGA Championship, Australian Open
1968   West End Open, Victorian Open
1971   New Zealand Open
1972   Australian Open
1973   Victorian Open

European Tour wins: 26

1954	News of the World Match Play, **The Open Championship**
1955	**The Open Championship**
1956	**The Open Championship**
1957	Yorkshire Evening News Tournament
1958	Dunlop Tournament (United Kingdom), Daks Tournament (tied with Harold Henning), **The Open Championship**
1959	Italian Open, Spanish Open
1960	Yorkshire Evening News Tournament, Daks Tournament, Bowmaker Tournament, German Open
1961	News of the World Match Play, British Masters, Esso Golden Tournament (tied with Dave Thomas)
1962	Piccadilly Tournament, Martini International
1965	Daks Tournament, **The Open Championship**
1966	News of the World Match Play
1967	News of the World Match Play, Alcan International
1968	British Masters
1970	Martini International (tie with Douglas Sewell)
1972	W.D. & H.O. Wills Tournament (United Kingdom)

Japan Golf Tour win

1976	Pepsi-Wilson Tournament

Other wins: eight

1954	Canada Cup (with Kel Nagle)
1959	Canada Cup (with Kel Nagle)
1960	Hong Kong Open
1964	Indian Open, Philippine Open
1965	Hong Kong Open
1966	Indian Open
1976	Indian Open

Senior majors: one

Senior PGA Tour wins: 11

1984   World Seniors Invitational, **Senior PGA Championship**

1985   Vintage Invitational, American Golf Classic, MONY Senior
Tournament of Champions, Champions Classic, Senior Players
Reunion Pro-Am, MONY Syracuse Senior's Classic, du Maurier
Champions, United Virgin Bank Seniors, Barnett Suntree Senior
Classic

CHAPTER 10

BILLY CASPER

Mr. Unflappable
got snubbed he should
have been in the Big Four

William Earl Casper Jr. was born June 24, 1931 in San Diego (age 83 as of this writing), is a forgotten golf legend who was, unofficially, one of the Big Four with Arnold Palmer, Jack Nicklaus and Gary Player, on the PGA Tour from the late 1950s to mid-1970s.

PGA Tour's equivalent of Rodney Dangerfield

Although Casper is recognized as a top player in the history of the PGA Tour, he hasn't received the recognition he deserves. Unfortunately for Billy, his contemporaries included three all-time legends of the game: Palmer, Nicklaus and Player. Casper made a huge blunder to leave his sports agent Mark McCormick early in his career, uncomfortable with McCormick's aggressive marketing style. If he had stayed with McCormick, he would have received due recognition and become known as one of the Big Four. In his 2012 book, *The Big Three and Me*, Billy calls himself an idiot for leaving McCormick—the first superstar sports agent.

The only knock on Casper's record, comparing him with the Big Three, who won a combined 34 majors (Nicklaus 18, Palmer seven and Player nine), is that he merely won three majors—making his total seem inadequate. It's surprising after winning the U.S. Open at the fairly young age of 28, he didn't win another major until he was 35 in 1966, at the U.S. Open again. That was the year he rallied from seven strokes back, during the final nine to tie Palmer, before beating him in the playoff. Billy put on quite a putting exhibition that week, with 33 one-putt greens and no three-putts in regulation play. However, that Open is probably better remembered for Arnie's collapse than for Billy's win.

There are several reasons why Casper didn't win a lot of majors. First, Billy was a bit overweight, likely making it difficult for him to maintain his stamina throughout the four pressure-packed rounds of a major. Nicklaus had slimmed down, Palmer stayed fit and Player became super-fit. Secondly, Casper was merely an average length driver of the golf ball and it's very difficult for a golfer who is not long off the tee to win a large number of many majors.

Regarding his major wins, historians seem to overlook that Billy's chances of winning the British Open were limited because he only played it five times—after waiting until he was 37 (in 1968) to play for the first time. Yet, in those few appearances, he made the cut every time and finished as high as fourth and seventh on two of those occasions. Thus, had Casper played in The Open Championship all of his prime years like Nicklaus, he probably would have won one or two.

Billy also reflected in *The Big Three* that he did not regard the majors as significantly as he should have—focusing on the steady money he was earning by playing a heavy schedule of weekly tour events, assuring enough earnings to provide for his large and growing family. Casper would have earned more money from endorsements if he had won more majors and fewer regular tour events. Nevertheless, Billy provided a very comfortable living for his family.

Casper's advantage over his competition

He's regarded as one of the best putters in the history of the game. The way Johnny Miller talks, no one else held a candle to Casper when it came to putting. Miller said Casper was known for doing things that were almost unbelievable.

Miller, who played a lot of golf with Casper, talked about how Billy expected to sink every makeable putt and frequently did.

But if he missed a putt he thought he should have holed, and was left with a 3-footer coming back, he would often purposely slam that 3-footer so hard it would hit the back of the hole, and pop up in the air before falling in. He seemed to punish the ball for not falling in on the first putt like it was supposed to. If he ever missed one of those, he would have had a lengthy putt coming back. But apparently Casper never missed! That's amazing. I've watched Tiger Woods, the only megastar of today, miss numerous 3-footers that were hit too hard and popped out of the hole—or miss the hole entirely.

Casper was highly skilled at working the ball on both his drives and approach shots—something you don't see much from tour players today. He would fade the ball with his driver and then either draw or fade his approach, whatever the shot required. Thus, in addition to his putting prowess, he had considerable shot-making skills. That's a tough combination to beat, even for a long-ball hitter who is, merely, a good shot-maker and putter.

It reminds me of short-hitting Zach Johnson soundly beating long-hitting Dustin Johnson, in head-to-head competition, to win 2014's opening PGA Tour event at Kapalua—despite the lengthy layout and wide-open fairways that should have provided a big advantage to Dustin. (Zach's possible advantage is that he wasn't hooked on cocaine at the time.)

"Billy just gave you this terrible feeling he was never going to make a mistake, and then he'd drive a stake through your heart with that putter. It was a very efficient operation," said Casper's close friend Dave Marr, the sportscaster and golf pro who died in 1997.

Choke-free

Unlike everyone else, Billy seemed to have no ego and never got nervous. According to Miller, "It didn't seem to bother him if you out-drove him or hit your approach shots inside of him. He would always maintain complete control of his emotions and prod along in a very business-like fashion. He knew that if he simply played error-free golf, he probably would beat you in the end—and he usually did."

Of all the greatest PGA Tour players since the 1940s, Billy Casper is the only golfer who never choked once in his career. Nicklaus, Woods, Hogan, Snead, Nelson, Palmer, Player, Trevino, Watson, Floyd—they all choked on multiple occasions. This is true particularly in putting—with Hogan, Snead, Nelson, Palmer and Watson fighting the yips.

Nicklaus admitted to shanking the ball on Augusta National's short par-3 12th hole during a Masters tournament, back in the 1960s. Floyd admitted to choking during his 1990 Masters playoff with Nick Faldo, when hitting his approach shot into the pond left of the green on Augusta's 11th hole—handing the tournament to Faldo. Player admitted to choking on the 72nd hole of the 1959 Open Championship, where he made a double-bogey and thought he had lost the tournament (yet he still won). In Trevino's case, even though he was renowned as one of the greatest ball-strikers of all time, he had more chipping and putting chokes than one could count. And Tiger, possibly the greatest golfer ever, seems to have as many chokes—since his fall from grace in 2009—as great shots, despite winning five tournaments in 2013.

But none of it happened to Billy—he never had the yips and he never choked! Johnny Miller and other tour players who played with Casper would attest to this. He was almost super-human.

I watched the final round of the 2014 Valspar Championship, won by John Senden, the only player who didn't choke, while his pursuers seemed to nearly choke to death. Robert Garrigus, who started out with a two-shot lead, choked terribly early in the round, leading to a horrendous score of 41 on the front side that quickly dashed his hopes of winning. Kevin Na, playing in the final group with Garrigus, choked noticeably, dropping four shots early on, before bouncing back and finishing second.

Justin Rose, reigning U.S. Open champion, choked so badly he looked like a 30-handicapper on one hole, where he laid the sod over the ball from a perfect lie in the middle of the fairway, losing control of his club and letting it fly out of his hands in the follow through—with a sand wedge, for crying out loud!

Young lefty Scott Langley, tied for the lead halfway through the final nine, had a chance before he gagged on a couple of short putts to kill his shot at winning. Even Luke Donald, who won this event in 2012, seemed to choke a bit coming down the stretch, missing a couple of short putts that blew his win.

All this took place in a single round of golf, while Casper never choked in his many thousands of rounds! That may be the most amazing career stat in the history of the PGA Tour, if not professional golf. So I ask the golf world, let's call Billy Casper "Mr. Unflappable."

Casper had 51 PGA Tour wins in his career, his first in 1956, placing him seventh on the all-time list. His victories helped him finish third in McCormack's World Golf Rankings in 1968, 1969 and 1970, the first three years they were published. He won three major championships: the 1959 and 1966 U.S. Opens, and the 1970 Masters Tournament. He was the PGA Tour Money Winner in 1966 and 1968. He was PGA Player of the Year in 1966 and 1970. Casper won the Vardon Trophy for lowest-scoring average five times: 1960, 1963, 1965, 1966 and 1968.

He was a member of the United States team in the Ryder Cup eight times: 1961, 1963, 1965, 1967, 1969, 1971, 1973, 1975 and a non-playing captain in 1979. Casper has scored the most points in the Ryder Cup by an American player. Casper won at least one PGA Tour event for 16 straight seasons, from 1956 to 1971. This is the third-longest streak, trailing only Palmer and Nicklaus, who each won on the Tour 17 straight years.

On the PGA Senior Tour, Casper won nine times from 1982 to 1989, including two senior majors. Casper was inducted into the World Golf Hall of Fame in 1978.

Quotes by and about Billy Casper

"Think ahead. Golf is a next-shot game."

"Try to think where you want to put the ball, not where you don't want it to go."

"Play every shot so that the next one will be the easiest that you can give yourself."

"He congratulated me...and I put my arm around him and said, 'I'm sorry.' At a time like that, you really feel for a fellow competitor. People

still focus on the total collapse of Arnie, but they don't realize I shot 32 on the back nine to force that playoff. There were only 15 rounds under par at Olympic in '66, and I had four of them."

"Golf puts a man's character on the anvil and his richest qualities— patience, poise and restraint—to the flame."

"Oh, I used to make 'em once in a while."

"What you do today can improve all your tomorrows."

"Set your sights high, the higher the better. Expect the most wonderful things to happen, not in the future but right now. Realize that nothing is too good. Allow absolutely nothing to hamper you or hold you up in any way."

"Believe you can and you're halfway there."

"Be more concerned with your character than with your reputation. Your character is what you really are, while your reputation is merely what others think you are."

"Change your thoughts and you change your world."

"I've learned that no matter what happens, or how bad it seems today, life does go on, and it will be better tomorrow. I've learned that you can tell a lot about a person by the way he/she handles these three things: a rainy day, lost luggage, and tangled Christmas tree lights. I've learned that regardless of your relationship with your parents, you'll miss them when they're gone from your life. I've learned that making a living is not the same thing as making a life. I've learned that life sometimes gives you a second chance. I've learned that you shouldn't go through life with a catcher's mitt on both hands; you need to be able to throw some things back.

I've learned that whenever I decide something with an open heart, I usually make the right decision. I've learned that even when I have pains, I don't have to be one. I've learned that every day you should reach out and touch someone. People love a warm hug, or just a friendly pat on the back. I've learned that I still have a lot to learn. I've learned that people will forget what you said, people will forget what you did, but people will never forget how you made them feel."

"Education is the ability to listen to almost anything without losing your temper."

"When you reach the end of your rope, tie a knot in it and hang on."

"If you listen to your fears, you will die never knowing what a great person you might have been."

"Whenever you're in conflict with someone, there is one factor that can make the difference between damaging your relationship and deepening it. That factor is attitude."

Johnny Miller: *"Billy has the greatest pair of hands God ever gave a human being."*

Lee Trevino: *"When I came up, I focused on Casper. I figured he was twice as good as me, so I watched how he practiced and decided I would practice three times as much as him."*

Billy Casper professional wins: 68
Major championship wins: three
1959   **U.S. Open**
1966   **U.S. Open**
1970   **Masters**

PGA Tour wins: 51

1956 Labatt Open

1957 Phoenix Open, Kentucky Derby Open

1958 Bing Crosby National Pro-Am, Greater New Orleans Open, Buick Open

1959 U.S. Open, Portland Centennial Open, Lafayette Open, Mobile Seritoma Open

1960 Portland Open Invitational, Hesperia Open Invitational, Orange County Open

1961 Portland Open Invitational

1962 Doral C.C. Open, Greater Greensboro Open, 500 Festival Open Invitational, Bakersfield Open Invitational

1963 Bing Crosby National Pro-Am, Insurance City Open

1964 Doral Open, Colonial National Invitation, Greater Seattle Open Invitational, Almaden Open Invitational, Bob Hope Desert Classic, Western Open, Insurance City Open Invitational, Sahara Invitational

1966 San Diego Open, U.S. Open, Western Open, 500 Festival Open Invitational

1967 Canadian Open, Carling World Open

1968 Los Angeles Open, Greater Greensboro Open, Colonial National Invitational, 500 Festival Open, Greater Hartford Open, Lucky International Open

1969 Bob Hope Desert Classic, Western Open, Alcan Open

1970 Los Angeles Open, The Masters, IVB-Philadelphia Golf Classic, AVCO Golf Classic

1971 Kaiser National Open Invitational

1973 Western Open, Sammy Davis Jr.-Greater Hartford Open

1975 First NBS New Orleans Open

European Tour win

1975 Italian Open

Other wins: six

1958 Brazil Open

1959	Brazil Open
1973	Hassan II Golf Trophy
1974	Trophée Lancôme (France, unofficial European Tour event)
1975	Hassan II Golf Trophy
1977	Mexican Open

Senior PGA Tour wins: nine
Senior major championship wins: two

1982	Shootout at Jeremy Ranch, Merrill Lynch/Golf Digest Commemorative Pro-Am
1983	**U.S. Senior Open**
1984	Senior PGA Tour Roundup,
1987	Del Webb Arizona Classic, Greater Grand Rapids Open
1988	Vantage at The Dominion, **Mazda Senior Tournament Players Championship**
1989	Transamerica Senior Golf Championship

Other senior win

1984	Liberty Mutual Legends of Golf (with Gay Brewer)
	Ryder Cup competition wins: nine for nine
	1961, 1963, 1965, 1967, 1969, 1971, 1973, 1975 (winners); **1979** (winners, non-playing captain)

CHAPTER 11

SEVE BALLESTEROS SOTA

*Amazing talent,
misnomered "hack"*

H ere's a photo of young Seve. He turned pro a month after his 17th birthday in 1974 but admitted years later this was the biggest mistake of his life, because he lost his childhood.

Severiano "Seve" Ballesteros Sota, April 9, 1957-May 7, 2011, died at 54. Seve was born in the village of Pedreña, Cantabria, Spain, the youngest of five boys of Baldomero Ballesteros Presmanes and Carmen Sota Ocejo. One sibling died in childhood; all the others became professional golfers.

This golf legend was a world No. 1 and a leading golf figure from the mid-1970s to the mid-'90s. He won more than 90 international tournaments in his career, including five majors between 1979 and 1988—The Open Championship three times and the Masters Tournament twice. He gained attention in the golfing world in 1976, when at 19 he finished second at The Open.

Ballesteros learned the game playing on the beaches near his home, while skipping school, using a 3-iron given him by his older brother Manuel when he was 8. Manuel finished in the top 100 on the European Tour Order of Merit from 1972 to 1983. Yet most Americans never heard of him. He later became Seve's manager. His other pro golf brothers were Vicente and Baldomero.

Seve burst onto the world golf scene in the 1976 Open Championship at Royal Birkdale Golf Club. He led by two shots after the third round. However, he received a schooling from Johnny Miller who began the final round two shots behind Seve. Miller closed with a blistering 66 to win by six, after Seve finished with a 74 that gave him a tie for second with Jack Nicklaus—which, for 19-year-old Seve, was an impressive performance.

Seve went on to win the European Money Title that year, earning a whopping £39,500. It's surprising how the European Tour played for paltry sums into the late '70s. Seve wound up winning the Money Title six times, including the following two years, which was a record at that time—until Colin "Monty" Montgomerie came along later, winning it seven years in a row from '93 to '99.

Seve captured his first major at The Open Championship in 1979 when he was just 22. He won by a margin of three over Jack Nicklaus and Ben Crenshaw at Royal Lytham & St Annes. This is the tournament where Seve hit his ball way off to the right on the 16th hole and made a birdie from the overflow parking lot. The ball came to rest under a car. After a free drop, Ballesteros played a sand wedge to the green, then sank the 30-foot birdie putt.

Most of the golf world seemed to believe that Seve simply hit a terribly wayward tee shot on that hole, but was incredibly lucky to wind up with a good lie and fairly easy shot to the green, after taking a drop from the parking lot. However, Seve contended that it was all part of his strategy and that he hit his tee shot there intentionally. In any case, this victory made him the youngest winner of the tournament in the 20th century, and the first golfer from continental Europe to win a major in over 70 years.

Ballesteros went on to win four additional majors—the Masters in 1980 and 1983, and The Open again in 1984 and 1988. Ballesteros described the putt he holed on the 18th green at St Andrews, winning the 1984 Open Championship, as "the happiest moment of my whole sporting life." Seve's 1980 Masters win was the first by a European player, and at the time he was the youngest winner of the tournament, at 23—until Tiger, at age 21, blew away the field by 12 in 1997.

In 1988, Ballesteros won his fifth and last major title, The Open at Royal Lytham & St Annes. The final round was played on Monday after heavy rainfall washed out Saturday's play. Ballesteros was at the top of his game in firing a final round of 65. He ended up winning by two strokes over Nick Price, and called it the greatest round of his life.

He played a leading role in the re-emergence of European golf, helping the European Ryder Cup team to five wins both as a player and captain. He won the World Match Play Championship a record-tying five times. Seve was widely known for his dashing and imaginative style of play, with a Houdini-like short game and erratic driving of the golf ball. However, golf analyst Nick Faldo once commented that if he had started driving the ball as wildly as Seve, he would have sued his coach, David Ledbetter. Nonetheless, Seve is generally regarded as the greatest European golfer outside the U.K. He won a record 50 times on the European Tour.

Not remembered kindly

Sadly, in the United States, Ballesteros has become somewhat forgotten by the 20-something golfers. Their most recent memory of Seve was his attempt to compete on the Champions Tour after turning 50 in 2007. He entered just one tournament, the Regions Charity Classic, in late May of that year and shot rounds of 78, 81, 73, which put him at +16 and in last place. Frankly, if it hadn't been for Seve's short-game wizardry, he would have had a hard time breaking 80 in that third round. But you have to admire a guy who can miss every fairway and half the greens, but still come mighty close to paring the course.

I spoke to a 25-year-old golfer who watched Seve play in his lone Senior Tour event, and he was not impressed. "That Ballesteros guy was such a hack," he said. "He couldn't hit the fairway if his life depended upon it. What does he have against playing out of the short grass?" Unfortunately, that was a brutal, but accurate assessment of Seve's game at the time. After that event, Ballesteros officially retired from golf—acknowledging that his game wasn't quite up to tournament competition. Seve was still the master of understatement.

Although Ballesteros bowed out of competitive golf gracefully, it tormented him to watch golfers nowhere near as talented as he was playing successful tournament golf into their 50s and even 60s. Deep down, he was bitter that these inferior golfers found success on the Senior Tour while he was forced to retire from the game at 50. Sadly, Seve died just four years later.

Enduring physical and mental struggle

Ballesteros began struggling with his form in the 1990s, due to back ailments, but stayed involved in golf, creating the Seve Trophy and entering the golf-course design business.

Ballesteros married Carmen Botín, daughter of wealthy Spanish banker Emilio Botín, who had an estimated net worth in 2005 equivalent to $1.7 billion. Seve and Carmen were together from 1988 until their divorce in 2004. The marriage reportedly got rocky when Seve had trouble accepting he had lost his game. Another problem was Seve's father-in-law saw professional golfers—Seve included—as glorified caddies. Being a proud man, that had to sting.

From the early 1980s to mid-1990s, Ballesteros played a commanding role on the European Ryder Cup team. He scored 22½ points in 37 matches against the U.S. team. Partnering with his young protégé, Jose María Olazabal, they became the most successful team in the history of the competition, with 11 wins and two halved matches out of 15 pair matches. During the years Ballesteros and Olazabal were a teamed, Europe won the Ryder Cup 66 percent of the time. They won the cup in 1985, retained it in 1987 and 1989, lost it in 1991 and 1993, and regained the cup in 1995.

The swan song of his career in competition came in 1997, when he captained the winning European side at Valderrama Golf Club in Spain. This was the first Ryder Cup ever held in Europe outside the U.K. The Europeans retained the cup that year, beating the U.S. 14½ to 13½ with Tom Kite as captain of the U.S. team. Prior to that Ryder Cup, the two captains, Ballesteros and Kite, played a friendly match against each other. But Kite won easily; Seve had lost his game by that time.

Ballesteros led the Official World Golf Ranking for 61 weeks, from April 1986 to September 1989. He also led McCormack's World Golf Rankings, published in McCormack's *World of Professional Golf* annuals (from which the official rankings were developed) in 1983, 1984 and 1985. He was consistently in the world's top 10 according to those rankings for 15 years, from 1977 to 1991.

Seve was inducted into the World Golf Hall of Fame in 1999 and introduced the Seve Trophy in 2000, a team competition similar to the Ryder Cup, pitting a team from Great Britain and Ireland against one from continental Europe. In

2000, Ballesteros was ranked as 16th greatest golfer of all time by *Golf Digest* magazine. That's about where I would rank Seve—an impressive career.

Heading into 2005, Ballesteros had been mostly out of competitive golf since the late 1990s, but wanted to re-enter tournament competition in 2006. After playing in just one event on the European Tour, where he missed the cut after shooting a pair of 81s, he entered The Open Championship at Royal Liverpool. Nick Faldo was stunned to learn that Seve was playing in The Open that year, thinking he had wisely retired from competitive golf. However, despite an erratic tee-to-green game he managed a 74 in his first round, a score he would never have admitted being proud of.

Had it not been for his magical short game, he would have had a hard time breaking 80. Nevertheless, his 74 was three strokes better than Faldo's 77. The second round of 77 was a reality check as he missed the cut, but still a respectable performance, considering his lengthy absence from competition in the majors. Seve managed to have the last laugh as Faldo proved to be an even worse hack.

Seve was looking forward to joining the Champions Tour and European Seniors Tour upon turning 50 in 2007. We know how that turned out. After further back problems, which contributed to his finishing dead last in his only Champions Tour start, Ballesteros announced his retirement from golf on July 16, 2007, bringing an end to his illustrious career. During the news conference, the media addressed rumors about a recent hospital stay following an attempted suicide. Seve denied that, saying the rumors "were not even close to reality." He had been briefly hospitalized for a possible heart condition, but, as it turned out, the problem was all in his head.

Seve's first major health alarm occurred at the Madrid Airport Oct. 6, 2008, when he lost consciousness and was admitted to a hospital. A week later, he confirmed that he was diagnosed with a malignant brain tumor. On Oct. 15, he underwent a grueling 12-hour operation to remove the tumor. It was the first of four surgeries on a massive cancerous growth.

Following the fourth operation, which took 6½ hours, it was announced that the tumor had finally been removed. Seve was discharged Dec. 9. He returned home to Pedreña, Cantabria, where he began chemotherapy. A month later, he informed his fans his health was improving.

"I am very motivated and working hard although I am aware that my recovery will be slow and therefore I need to be patient and have a lot of determination. For these reasons I am following strictly all the instructions that the doctors are giving me. Besides, the physiotherapists are doing a great job on me and I feel better every day."

Seve required chemo until April of 2009. In his first public appearance since the tumor diagnosis, he called it a miracle to be alive and thanked all his care providers.

On May 6, 2011, Ballesteros' family released the news that his neurological condition had taken a turn for the worse. He died shortly afterwards, in the early hours of May 7, 2011.

The Open de España was underway when Ballesteros died. The European Tour marked his death with a moment of silence during the third round at the Real Club de Golf El Prat in Barcelona. In light of Seve's celebrity status in Spain, they should have held at least a day of mourning! I'll never forget the outcry of grief following Payne Stewart's death in that airplane disaster. The PGA Tour's tribute to Payne in the U.S. was a whole lot more than a moment of silence. I recall it going on for days, with bagpipes, lengthy speeches from close

Here's Seve winning his second major and first of two Masters, at 23

friends, players wearing knickers in his memory, endless conversations about the life of Payne Stewart and a documentary of his short life.

But with Seve's death, the sentiment seemed to be "to hell with him, let's get on with this week's competition." Ballesteros was cremated and his ashes scattered around his home estate.

Seve won the 1980 Masters by four shots over Gibby Gilbert and Jack Newton. Young Seve played the front nine of the final round in masterful fashion, reminiscent of Nicklaus at his very best. He began the fourth round with a seven-stroke lead and increased it to 10, after nine holes. It looked like a boring, blowout victory which had never been seen before at the Masters. Seve was nice enough, though, to give us a bit of suspense by plunking balls in the water on both Amen Corner holes 12 and 13, dramatically reducing his lead from 10 to three.

However, after paring the 14th hole, Seve managed to right the ship with a birdie on 15 and pars on the final three holes—giving him a fairly comfortable four-stroke margin victory.

In the photo we have Fuzzy Zoeller, the 1979 Masters champion, sliding the Masters jacket on Seve, who had to be the most popular golfer in the world at that moment. I vividly recall watching the final round of that tournament in the Palm Springs Country Club and one of my cohorts commenting, at the conclusion of the front nine, how Seve was the coolest golfer in the world and didn't have a nerve in his body—to which none of the dozen golfers in attendance disagreed.

Seve's hiccups, during the final nine, tell us he was either very human or proving he could butcher a couple holes in a row on the back nine and still waltz away with an easy victory. Only a moron would do something like that on purpose. But it worked out well for Seve, so I'm not knocking it.

Seve's Golf Swing

The photo of Seve's follow-through (on the next page) was taken early in his career by U.K. photographer Andrew Arthur—whom Seve glared at after this picture was taken, thinking he was too close to the tee box. In light of his exaggerated reverse-C finish, it's no wonder he developed crippling back problems later in life.

Ballesteros was the ultimate "feel" player. Here's what David Ledbetter had to say about how it influenced Seve's wedge play: "I've watched that guy over the years, and I know there are a lot of great wedge players, like Tom Kite and others. But I would ask Seve, 'Do you know exactly how far that is?'

"He would say, 'I see it. I feel it. I hit it.' It was just incredible how he was so attached to the hole. His distance control, it was amazing. He had only a 56-degree and a pitching wedge. What he was able to do with those two clubs was just incredible. He's the best wedge player I've seen in the modern era."

The great thing about being a feel player is he never had to worry about swing mechanics, as long is the feel was there. However, when he lost his feel, he had no mechanics to fall back on. As he became desperate to get his game back, he started thinking mechanically and listening to swing coaches, whom he had previously distrusted. At that point, Ballesteros was in big trouble. He became a poster child for the feel player who tries to become mechanical, and never regained his winning form.

Seve's last hurrah came in October of 2009, a year after his brain tumor diagnosis. He was awarded the Lifetime Achievement Award for the second time at the BBC Sports Personality Awards. Seve granted an interview with BBC golf commentator Peter Alliss shortly afterward. In this poignant interview Seve touched on his struggle through the past year. But he was upbeat and positive. He told his many fans in the U.K. not to feel sorry for him, claiming he was "the luckiest man alive. This thing that happened to me is a very little thing compared to other people who have tougher times." Speaking from his home in northern Spain, he added, "I've had a very good life."

Realizing his days on earth were near the end, he spoke with a hint of sadness in his eyes. "I'm sure that some people will feel sorry for me or maybe cry when they see this program. But I feel very happy and a very lucky person because throughout my life I have had so many great moments and I feel that I lived two or three more lives than the average person. I don't want people to feel sorry for me. I've had so much luck and so much fun for so many years."

Seve admitted his medical treatments were brutal. "Patience has never been my strongest point and to spend 22 days in intensive care and 72 days in one room, you need tremendous patience....Life is like sport. You have to fight every day and the key is never give up. If you pull the white handkerchief, like Hale Irwin, you never win."

That last comment sounded off, considering how Irwin is the most winning golfer in Senior Tour history with 45 wins—a record that no Senior/Champions Tour golfer will come close to catching. Seve quit after his first Senior Tour event. I'm not suggesting he made the wrong decision to hang it up. However, it was wacky for Seve to suggest that Irwin was a quitter. But one thing I always loved about Seve is he never hesitated to say something that was on his mind, no matter how idiotic or controversial.

Seve endured suffering in his final years with bravery. I especially like his quote, "Life is like golf and you have to play it as it lies." Or was it Bobby Jones who said that?

The loss of Seve at a young age was an international tragedy. Despite his display of gamesmanship, temper outbursts and histrionics on the golf course—or because of those things—whenever Seve was in contention, it was always fun watching him play. He faced death calmly and fearlessly. The courage and dignity through which Seve lived his final days was inspirational.

Quotes by and about Seve Ballesteros

"I'd like to see the fairways more narrow. Then everyone would have to play from the rough, not just me."

"Ask the American players how many weeks in a row they play in Japan."

"Yeah, but I'll be working as a marshal. I'll be helping your team find all the balls they drive into the rough."

"No Trevino speaks Mexican."

"I look into their eyes, shake their hand, pat their back, and wish them luck, but I am thinking, 'I am going to bury you.'"

"I don't see any players who really today impress me from either side of the Atlantic, to be honest. There are a lot of players with great talent and a great future ahead. But impress me? I don't get impressed that easily."

"I miss, I miss, I make."

"I'm here because golf is my sport and I like to compete....Just by being here I'm already beginning to win."

"It is very sad. I was treated with disrespect. It was hard to sleep, and I cried because the players' committee judged me without regard for the big picture and my contributions to the European tour."

"My intention is to compete until I'm 54. So if I join the Champions Tour, it will only be for four years—no more than that." [You were only off by four years, Seve.]

David Ledbetter: *"He was totally illogical. I had to fight through his personality to get him to do what I wanted him to do. I could never just tell him what to do. I always had to make him think everything was his idea. I'd manipulate him until he'd suggest something and I would immediately agree....*

"He was amazing to work with though, a genius. I've never seen anyone with such skill, especially with wedges. He had shots no one else had. He had control over the ball like no one else. The new balls killed off his edge though."

Seve Ballesteros professional wins: 91

Major championship wins: five

1979	The Open Championship
1980	The Masters
1983	The Masters
1984	The Open Championship
1988	The Open Championship

European Tour wins: 50

1976   Dutch Open

1977   Open De France, Uniroyal International Championship, Swiss Open

1978   Martini International, German Open, Scandinavian Open, Swiss Open

1979   Lada English Golf Classic, **The Open Championship**

1980   **The Masters**, Madrid Open, Martini International, Dutch Open

1981   Scandinavian Open, Spanish Open

1982   Madrid Open, Paco Rabanne Open de France

1983   **The Masters**, Sun Alliance PGA Championship, Irish Open, Lacome Trophy

1984   **The Open Championship**

1985   Irish Open 25, Puegeot Open de France, Sanyo Open, Spanish Open

1986   Dunhill British Masters, Irish Open, Monte Carlo Open, Peugeot Open de France, Dutch Open, Lancombe Trophy

1987   Suze Open

1988   Mallorca Open de Baleares, The Open Championship, Scandinavian Open, German Open, Lancome Trophy

1989   Madrid Open, Grand Prix of Europe Matchplay Championship, Swiss Masters

1990   Open Renault de Baleares

1991   Volvo PGA Championship, Dunhill British Masters

1992 Dubia Desert Classic, Turespana Open de Baleares

1994 Benson & Hedges International Open, German Masters

1995 Spanish Open

PGA Tour wins: nine

1978 Greater Greensboro Open

1979 **The Open Championship, The Masters**

1983 **The Masters**, Westchester Classic

1984 **The Open Championship**

1985 New Orleans Classic

1988 Westchester Classic, **The Open Championship**

Japan Golf Tour wins: six

1977 Japan Open, Dunlop Phoenix

1978 Japan Open,

1981 Dunlop Phoenix

1988 Visa Taiheiyo Masters

1991 The Crowns

Other wins: 31

1974 Spanish National Championship for under 25s, Open de Vizcaya

1975 Spanish National Championship for under 25s

1976 Memorial Donald Swaelens, Cataluña Championship, Tenerife Championship, Lancome Trophy, World Cup of Golf (with Manuel Piñero)

1977 Otago Classic (New Zealand), Braun International Golf (Germany), World Cup ofGolf (with Antonio Garrido)

1978 Kenya Open, Spanish National Championship for under 25s

1979 Open el Prat

1981 Australian PGA Championship, Suntory World Match Play Championship (England)

1982 Masters de San Remo (Italy), Suntory World Match Play Championship (England)

1983 Million Dollar Challenge (South Africa)

1984   Suntory World Match Play Championship (England), Million Dollar Challenge (South Africa)

1985   Spanish Championship for Professionals, Suntory World Match Play Championship (England), Campeonato de España-Codorniu

1987   APG Larios, Campeonato de España Para Professionales

1988   APG Larios

1991   Toyota World Match Play Championship (England)

1992   Copa Quinto Centenario per Equipos, Fifth Centenary Cup (team)

1995   Tournoi Perrier de Paris (with José María Olazábal)

Team appearances

Ryder Cup (representing Europe)

1979, 1983; 1985, 1987 (winners); **1989** (tied, cup retained); **1991, 1993; 1995** (winners); **1997** (winners—non-playing captain)

World Cup (representing Spain)

1975; 1976, 1977 (winners); **1991**

Dunhill Cup (representing Spain)

1985, 1986, 1988

Double Diamond

1975, 1976, 1977

Hennessy Cognac Cup

1976, 1978, 1980

Seve Trophy

2000   (winners – playing captain); **2002, 2003** (playing captain); **2005, 2007** (non-playing captain)

Royal Trophy

2006, 2007 (winners – non-playing captain)

CHAPTER 12

JOHNNY MILLER

Yes, he played golf too

T his is a photo of Johnny when he was young and mean, doing his best Clint Eastwood impression. I think he's saying to his caddie, "In all the excitement, I kind of lost track. Did I hit four shots or just three?"

Johnny was born April 29, 1947, and is 66 years old—already, as of this writing. He was ranked second in Mark McCormack's World Golf Rankings in both 1974 and 1975, behind Jack Nicklaus. Annoyingly for Johnny, he always seemed to be in Jack's shadow.

You're probably thinking, "Everybody knows who he is." That may be true. However, I recently asked an avid golfer in his mid-20s named Danny what he knew about Johnny Miller. "Oh, he's my favorite golf announcer," Danny said. "I love the way he calls everything exactly the way he sees it and never holds any punches. Over the years, there have only been a couple times, I can recall, where he made comments that were totally out of line.

"Back in 2004 for example, during the Doral Open, Johnny made the comment that Ben Hogan would puke if he saw Craig Parry's swing. I thought, wow, that's harsh. And that can't be true because, during Hogan's day, I don't believe there were many players (if any) who had swing coaches. So there must have been a lot of tour players, back then, who had uglier swings than Craig Parry.

"What made Johnny's comment even worse is that Parry went on to win the tournament that week, in a playoff on the 18th hole, one of the toughest holes on tour. He holed out a fairly long iron shot from the fairway for an eagle. It was an amazing golf shot—one of the best I've ever seen in my life. After he hit the shot, I could just see Parry saying, 'Take that Johnny Miller, you S.O.B.' But hey, I'd much rather listen to Johnny Miller than some wimpy, politically correct golf announcer who bores me to tears."

Danny knew a lot about Johnny Miller, the announcer. But almost nothing about Johnny Miller, the superstar golfer of the '70s. Danny couldn't name a single PGA Tour event that Johnny won. I was shocked that Danny wasn't at least familiar with Miller's '73 U.S. Open win. Most avid golfers know, only too well, that Johnny never fails to brag how he fired the greatest round in the history of golf, during the final day of that Open. But the fact that Johnny's announcing career has exceeded the length of his playing career causes a lot of people to view him as just an announcer.

What most people don't realize is that Johnny was probably the most talented ball striker in the history of the PGA Tour, aside from Ben Hogan. By his own admission, he was a lousy putter and spent very little time on the practice range after his mid-20s. He cut back his tournament play in his mid-30s before transitioning into announcing. Despite his limited play and practice schedule, Johnny managed to win 25 PGA Tour events and another 12 tournaments internationally. This included two majors—the U.S. Open and British Open.

However, Johnny was most impressive when he blew away the field in the 1975 Phoenix Open by a whopping 14 strokes and then followed that up, the very next week, by winning the Tucson Open by nine shots. It's one thing to take down the field with incredible putting, but Johnny did it knocking down the pins to take the pressure off his woeful putting. Johnny's most amazing round of golf, in tournament competition, was the final round of the 1973 U.S. Open when he charged from six behind, shooting an incredible 63 to win by a stroke—again with mediocre putting, which included a three-putt green from about 20 feet. I rank this a top-10 major championship win in PGA Tour history.

But his lack of dedication to the game and lousy putting prevented him from winning no more than two majors. It's damn near impossible to be a dedicated family man as he was purported to be, with six kids, and a dedicated PGA Tour professional. As Johnny reached his mid-30s, his putting got worse and worse. That's enough to drive anyone off the Tour and into the announcers' booth.

Johnny joined the PGA Tour in 1969 at 22, and won his first tour event in 1971. He managed just one more win by the end of 1972 at the Heritage Classic.

Coming into the 1973 U.S. Open at the difficult par-71 Oakmont layout, Miller was a 26-year-old with just two tour victories in four years, but had done well in several majors. He tied for second at the 1971 Masters, and had top-10 finishes at the U.S. Open in 1971 and 1972. Miller had yet to win in 1973, but by mid-June he had recorded eight top-10 finishes, which included a tie for sixth at the Masters.

Miller played the first two rounds at Oakmont with Arnie and his heavily blue-collar "army" at its largest in his home state. Miller was 2-under par (140) after the second round, but shot a 5-over 76 on Saturday to put himself at 3-over (216) for the championship—seemingly out of contention.

Miller played the front nine without his yardage book on Saturday until his wife, Linda, retrieved it for him. How could he forget something so important? Wasn't Johnny's caddie supposed to be on top of that? Don't tell me Andy forgot his yardage book too! I can imagine Johnny asking Andy, on that front nine on Saturday, "What club should I hit?" And Andy replies, "It beats me. *You* forgot the yardage book!"

Miller began the final-round six shots behind the four co-leaders, which included Palmer. Teeing off about an hour ahead of the final group, Miller shot his sizzling 8-under 63. He finished early and passed the top players of the day, Nicklaus, Palmer, Player and Trevino who finished behind him. Miller's 63 remains the lowest final round to win a major.

Miller birdied the first four holes and hit all 18 greens in regulation. He got five more birdies with only one bogey (a three-putt on No. 8—a 244-yard par-3), and needed 29 putts during the round—a lot of putts considering how he had birdie opportunities on practically every hole. Ten of his approach shots finished within 10 feet of the cup. In 2007, Miller said, modestly, "It was the greatest ball-striking round I've ever seen and I've been around a little bit."

Miller wound up at 5-under (279), winning the championship by a single stroke over John Schlee—who would never be heard from in the golf world again. Only six players, including Johnny, shot under par in the final round. His 63 must have been unbelievable to the rest of the field. Miller made $35,000 for that victory.

Miller followed his U.S. Open victory by finishing in a tie for second at the next major, The Open at Royal Troon a month later, three strokes behind champion Tom Weiskopf. (Weiskopf would go on to give the name Troon to his most famous course design so that people would remember his one and only major victory.) The tie for second here, by Johnny, was the start of five consecutive top-10 finishes for him at The Open.

In 1974, Miller was the leading money winner on the PGA Tour with eight victories and amassed a then-record $353,201 (not exceeded until 1978), and dethroned Nicklaus in becoming the Tour's leading money winner for the year.

Miller began 1975 with consecutive blow-out victories in the Phoenix and Tucson Opens. Miller later spoke, humbly, about his peak period in the mid-1970s: "When I won at Tucson by nine shots in 1975, I would say the average iron shot I hit that week was no more than 2 feet off line. It was unbelievable. When I was at my peak, I would go into streaks where I felt that I could knock down the pin from anywhere with my irons. I played some golf that I think is unequaled."

Johnny finished second to Nicklaus at the 1975 Masters, and third at The Open Championship later in the year at Carnoustie, just a single stroke from playoffs in both. Coming in second or third too often kept Johnny's total major count lower than it should have been—at just two.

In 1976, Miller won his second and final major at The Open Championship at Royal Birkdale with a final round 66. He won by six over Nicklaus and a 19-year-old Seve who had led by two after three rounds, before a final round 74 killed his chances—especially following the 66 by Miller. The course played hard and fast from scorching hot conditions in England that summer, during the 1976 U.K. heat wave that included fires breaking out during the tournament.

Miller's final round of 66 at Royal Birkdale tied the course record. Did Johnny's sizzling round of 66 ignite the fires?

Following his 1976 British Open win, Miller lost his game badly and failed to win for the next three years, due partly to the yips. But that wasn't the only problem. For endorsement reasons, Johnny also switched irons from the old forged MacGregor Tommy Armour Silver Scot's, which had worked so beautifully for him, to a set of Spalding cast irons with a different feel all wrong for Johnny. The club change made it impossible for him to execute shots he was able to hit with the forged Armour irons.

Between Miller's putting yips and his equipment debacle, his game was in tatters. He fell into such a slump in the late '70s he considered quitting the Tour. But Nicklaus, sort of a father figure, gave Johnny the inspiration he needed to hang in there and battle through it.

Miller didn't score another win until the winter of 1980 at the Jackie Gleason Inverrary Classic. In 1981, however, Johnny's game improved to the point of winning twice on the PGA Tour—the Tucson and LA Opens. The year was capped off with a win in the Sun City Million Dollar Challenge. He wound up being that year's leading worldwide money winner in golf.

Johnny would go on to win four more times in his career, the last in 1994. That final win was his most improbable, after stepping out of the announcer's booth with very little practice. He finished his career with 25 PGA Tour wins and 105 top-10 finishes. He was runner-up three times at the Masters in 1971, 1975 and 1981. The only major championship in which Miller failed to have a top-three finish is the PGA. He played on two Ryder Cup teams, 1975 and 1981. He was inducted into the World Golf Hall of Fame in 1998.

Johnny's stellar Senior Tour career never happened

Although Miller became eligible for the Senior Tour in 1997, he decided to forgo playing due to golf injuries to his knees, back, elbows, shoulders and wrists. "It's a brutal sport," he said. (I suppose that's why, after suffering a knee injury in 7th grade football, Andy North's doctor recommended he take up golf!)

Johnny recalls hitting his first practice balls at age 5—200 balls a day! As a pro, he hit 600 balls a day and estimates that he hit 7 million balls over 20 years! He says most of those balls were hit with high-powered swings that put tremendous stress on his back and joints. All 5-year-olds hit 200 balls a day, right?

Miller did a lot of ranch work (for some idiotic reason) that involved heavy lifting. (Johnny mentioned this to Count Yogi, in 1977 at the Los Angeles Open, and Yogi correctly predicted the end of Johnny's game.) Johnny also loved to race cars, motorcycles and virtually anything he could find to drive fast. In addition to that, he did a lot of partying and, apparently, heavy drinking. According to Johnny, that led to multiple crashes. What's funny is Dave Hill's 1977 book, *Teed Off*, describes Johnny Miller as "Mr. Clean" and mentions that he doesn't drink. Johnny sure fooled him.

In lieu of playing Senior Tour golf, Miller accepted an offer in 1990, at 43, to become the lead golf analyst for NBC Sports. NBC keeps trying to fire Johnny, but they're unable drag him away from the announcer's booth. They tried wild horses, but even that didn't work. Johnny keeps screaming, "I won't go, I won't go!" It's not a pretty sight. But his perseverance is impressive.

Quotes by Johnny Miller
(with astute commentary by yours truly)

"I don't want to brag but..." Don't lie, Johnny. Everybody knows you love to brag.

"Serenity is knowing that your worst shot is still pretty good." I'm guessing during the late '70s, Johnny had no serenity whatsoever.

"If I had been in the gallery, I'd have gone home." Let's face it, Johnny, a lot of golf fans wish you would leave the announcer's booth and go home.

"Only one golfer in a million grips the club lightly enough." Ironically, that one golfer happens to be Johnny Miller.

"The top American players have stunk it up." Don't be too harsh, Johnny. After all, Dave Hill in Teed Off talks about how you were a

bit of a choker early in your career, and you hit a shank in your first PGA Tour playoff. That had to be embarrassing. I shanked a shot once and I couldn't find a hole deep enough to jump into—and I happened to be hitting balls into the Grand Canyon. People down below were not happy campers.

"In some ways Tiger has been slightly cheated in his career by not having tougher guys to compete against, like me. On Sunday, if Tiger went up against me, he'd know deep down, Johnny's going to kick his butt if he doesn't play his best. And I don't believe he thinks that way now. He knows if he's playing good, he's got it."

"If Ben Hogan saw Craig Parry's swing, he'd puke." Ouch!

"Craig Parry's swing looks more like that of a 15-handicapper than a pro golfer." Johnny, I'm thinking it's not a good idea to disrespect a successful Aussie touring pro like Parry—particularly not the same week he wins the fricken tournament!

"Rocco Mediate looks like the guy who cleans Tiger Woods' pool"—in the nude, I would add.

"You don't see a name like Rocco on a U.S. Open trophy." We almost did. But we never will now—especially after Johnny jinxed him. The fact that Rocco is in his 50s as of this writing doesn't help his chances a hell of a lot, either. It also would help Rocco if he was able to carry his drives more than 200 yards.

"Good thing Tiger Woods isn't going to win today or else the USGA would ban backward hats." That typifies the USGA's rulings—like their stupid ban an anchored putting strokes.

"That ball could have been a foot from the hole if it had the right distance." Johnny, did you figure that out all by yourself?

"I'm usually thought to be full of hot air, but ..." I don't care to hear excuses as to why you're full of hot air.

"Plenty of people think golf commentary should be all positive. Clearly, I disagree." But it doesn't have to be all be negative either. Actually, I take that back. Once, after a player made an albatross, I believe Johnny said that his shot wasn't too bad.

"Tiger has the ability to make people feel uncomfortable, but not because he's not a nice guy. That's the mark of a truly phenomenal player. You can just feel he's better than you, and he knows he's better than you. That just widens the gap, though he doesn't say anything."

"If Tiger had played against me in my prime, I'm the one golfer he would never have intimidated." Sure, Johnny, we all know that you're the only golfer in the history of the game who Tiger wouldn't have intimidated.

On Tiger: *"Why didn't he hit the 'stinger'? That was the shot he needed. He has changed his swing so many times he has forgotten how."*

"Tiger's the guy I'd like to help most. I've been watching him since he was in junior golf. I know all the swings he's had. I think I could help him get back to his natural swing, not the swing someone else wants him to make. I'm open to helping him." Actually, Tiger told me he's looking for a new swing instructor with an even bigger ego than Johnny Miller. Good luck, Tiger.

"Tiger's not intimidating anymore, as a golfer. Everybody on tour knows they can beat him now—probably even the rookies." Johnny, you left out the college and high school golfers.

"Adam Scott will have to switch from his broomstick to a different putter when the new rule goes into effect in a couple years." I laugh at

that comment. Johnny has no clue how easy it will be to circumvent the anchored putting ban, scheduled for 2016.

"The pre-shot routine used to be one sentence. Now it's a paragraph." Johnny never had a chance to watch Cary Middlecoff play at his "glacially slow" pace. If Middlecoff had been any worse, he'd have been almost as slow as (six-hour) Andrew Loupe. Maybe Andrew's improved his pace since I last saw him—he couldn't have gotten any slower than he was in the 2014 Texas Open, in which he was penalized for slow play.

Johnny Miller professional wins: 32
Major championship wins: two

1973	**U.S. Open**
1976	**British Open**

PGA Tour wins: 25

1971	Southern Open Invitational
1972	Heritage Classic
1973	**U.S. Open**
1974	Bing Crosby, National Pro-Am, Phoenix Open, Tucson Open, Heritage Classic, Tournament of Champions, Westchester Classic World Open Golf Championship, Kaiser International Open
1975	Phoenix Open (by 14 strokes), Tucson Open (nine strokes), Bob Hope Desert Classic, Kaiser International
1976	Tucson Open, Bob Hope Desert Classic, The Open Championship
1980	Jackie Gleason Inverrary Classic
1981	Tucson Open, Los Angeles Open
1982	San Diego Open
1983	Honda Inverrary Classic
1987	Pebble Beach National Pro-Am
1994	Pebble Beach National Pro-Am

European Tour win
1979   Trophée Lancôme

Japan Tour win
1974   Dunlop Phoenix

Other wins: five
1973   Trophée Lancôme (France, unofficial European Tour event), World Cup (team title with Jack Nicklaus and individual title)
1981   Million Dollar Challenge (South Africa – unofficial event)
1983   Chrysler Team Championship (with Jack Nicklaus), Spalding Invitational

Professional team appearances
Ryder Cup: **1975, 1981** (winners)
World Cup: **1973** Teamed with Nicklaus (winners, individual winner); **1975** Teamed with Lou Graham (winners, individual winner); **1980** Remarkably, in two out of three World Cup appearances, not only did Johnny's team win (with both Jack Nicklaus and Lou Graham) but he won individual honors in both as well.

CHAPTER 13

Introducing the
greatest golfer ever—

COUNT YOGI

Guinness Book missed greatest round of golf

A ccording to the Count Yogi ® Golf website based on thousands of newspaper archives and written testimonials, Guinness totally missed the boat on the greatest round of golf ever played. Reportedly, in 1934 an enormously gifted golfer, going by the name of Harry M. Frankenberg, aka Count Yogi, shot a 55 at Bunker Hill Golf Course, winning the Chicago Golf Championship on a regulation length course, a par 74. This was accomplished, with the primitive equipment of the time, by Yogi shooting two back to back holes in one (on a par 3, 187 and a par 4, 347 yards)!!! The odds of doing so are 1 in 63 million. His playing partners that day included Al Espinosa, winner of 9 PGA Tour events and a pro named Terry McGovern. Count Yogi also holds the fastest played—lowest scored 9 holes in history; 9 under par 26 on a par 35 done in 58 minutes walking, not running!!!

Who was Count Yogi?

He is a man who was born in America just after the turn of the century. His ancestral background is quite unique. His ancestors include the legendary Chief Sitting Bull of the Sioux nation and his warrior son, Chief Gall. Born into poverty and blessed with an IQ of 185, he rose from poverty through intelligence, toughness, street smarts, and tenacious entrepreneurial efforts.

Divinely gifted with a Jim Thorpe type of athletic skill and ability of most sports, his primary choice and passion was golf. No one knew what Yogi's real name was, since American Indians don't have surnames like our European ancestors. So, when born he was given the European "blueblood" surname of his Bavarian grandmother on his father's side of Harry Hilary "Montana" Von Frankenberg (the "von" was dropped later to Americanize it).

He was known originally as the "Great Frankenberg" back in the early days of golf in America when the city of Chicago was considered the golf capital of that era. This was long before televised professional golf, as we know it today. Back then; all the top people in their fields were members of his two block long indoor health and golf school. It was featured in countless newspaper articles and on local radio shows, talking of members feeling

Harry M. Frankenberg, (AKA Count Yogi ®) in the News ©
© copyright Shell Castle Enterprises, All rights reserved
Hall of Fame Photo 1941, Encyclopedia Britannica, "Who's – Who"

healthier and happier with more vitality, while also dramatically improving and enjoying their golf games.

Much of Count Yogi's life is shrouded in mystery, but there's no doubt about his ability to play and teach the game.

In the 1939 photo on the next page, Count Yogi demonstrates his "physical and mental golf art technique." Watching is Lew Waldron, publicity chairman of the PGA (seated), and an audience including Walter Hagan, "Wild" Bill Melhorn, Tommy Armour, Babe Didrikson, Al Espinosa and Ben Hogan, then a student of Yogi's. Yogi displayed his revolutionary system of golf made easy for all, proving what he preached.

Harry M. Frankenberg (April 4th, ca 1908 – February 15th, 1990. *Photo Source: Published in "Revolutionary Golf Made Easy", 1941.*), AKA **Count Yogi** ®, a performing stage name given to him in the early 1950's by some of Hollywood's elite. He originally arrived in the Los Angeles area from Chicago, his boyhood town in 1949. Yogi had already experienced years of jealousy of his golfing talents, feats, and scoring ability. This is beside the fact that he had already played against golf's greats of that era and had beat all of them head to head. He also taught many of them to become champions. But his Jewish last name along with his indifference to the PGA's attempt to enforce only one way of teaching, he found himself being banned and racially discriminated from the PGA and even open tournaments. That forced him to become a golf performer and preacher/entertainer and form a miracle shot "Road-Show" which consisted of a non-stop hour and half long performance, followed up by an 18-hole playing/scoring exhibition with the pro, and the men and ladies club champions.

Adopting the stage name of "Count Yogi", he became like a Johnny Appleseed; traveling all over the united states of America, parts of Canada, Mexico and a few other destinations around the globe preaching what he called his *"Creator given, Infallible physical and mental routine."*

Headlines
Excerpts from Frankenberg's book, *Revolutionary Golf Made Easy* ©

- FRANKENBERG, A BOY OF 15, SHOOTS 69 IN TRIALS: WORLD'S YOUNGEST TUTOR & STYLIST
- FRANKENBERG'S 29-26—55 BREAKS WORLD'S COMPETITIVE 18-HOLE SCORING RECORD ON PAR 74 COURSE. DONE WITH TWO IN A ROW, BACK TO BACK HOLES IN ONES. THE ODDS ARE 1 IN 63 MILLION!!!
- HARRY FRANKENBERG SCORES PHENOMENAL 61 ON PAR 36-38—74 GOLF COURSE
- HARRY M. FRANKENBERG, UNSUNG HERO OF GOLFDOM PROFESSIONALS
- FRANKENBERG, REVOLUTIONARY THEORIST, TEACHES BLIND TO BREAK 100 FIRST TIME
- FRANKENBERG PLAYS AS HE TEACHES AND TEACHES AS HE PLAYS

Frankenberg has been acclaimed the most perfect mechanical golfer in the world. He says, "It isn't always what'd you shoot? It's how'd you shoot it?!" You'll find that whether Harry shoots his record low 55 or 75, he'll look the same on any day and with every shot, from the strokes to the drive. Hand skill and luck for the round will determine his score, not bad swinging or variety of form. If Harry uses one hand left or right, one leg, cross-handed, or any kind of stance or grip, he'll look excellent by just using his own system the same way he gives it to you in this publication. He'll hook or slice for you and look just the same to the naked eye as when he hits them straight. He'll play sandpit shots that will amaze you. This is his *"Revolutionary Golf Made Easy"* ©— no wiggles, waggles, lookups, look-backs, foot moves, shifts, twists, turns, wrist actions, left arming, left hand gripping, right elbow in, hitting down, inside outs, club shaft parallel, clubhead horizontal, or head down stuffed with anatomy at all. Harry says, "You play mentally right when you pull the clubhead back smoothly away from your body, and then control the clubhead by circling it around under the ball going to your body perfection follow-through—or you play mentally wrong.

HARRY FRANKENBERG, aka COUNT YOGI ®, HAS REVOLUTIONIZED THE SYSTEM OF TEACHING GOLF

Harry M. Frankenberg has taught more golfers per hour, per day, per year than anyone else.

Photo 1: Harry as a 15-year old pro scoring in the 60s in tournaments

Photo 2: Harry (right), the world's longest driver, and was Pro at Sportsman after the legendary Al Espinosa to his right

Photo 3: Harry as the greatest scorer, after scoring 203 rounds with an average of 67.7 shots per round in 1940

Photo 4: Harry the golf instructor, authority, critic and perfectionist— acclaimed by pros and amateurs as the "greatest golf authority of all"

Harry of 1935, teaching Mike Austin, renouned driving champion

Mike Austin was credited by Guinness World Records with hitting the longest drive in tournament play (471m/515 yards) in 1974 at Winterwood Golf Course (the Par-4 455-yard 14th Hole now called Desert Rose Golf Course) in Las Vegas, Nevada. The ball finished 65 yards past the flagstick. He accomplished this incredible feat at age 64!!! He used a Wilson 43.5-inch, steel-shafted persimmon driver and a 100-compression Titleist balata golf ball.

The proof is in the swing

Yogi was the real thing. The proof *isn't found* in research and signed documents of his spectacular feats, the proof is found in his perfect swing (film footage), the proof is found in Yogi's character, the proof is found in his never ending unbelievable trick shots, the proof is found in Mohammad Ali (who states on film that Yogi is the «greatest») and all the other famous athletes, politicians, actors, etc. that Yogi taught throughout the years. The proof is all around you. Just take a look at all the message boards and blogs currently on the internet, they run amuck with: interest, testimonials, enthusiasm, intrigue and much curiosity about the many accomplishments and the mysterious history of The Count.

Count Yogi has been gone for many years, but the public interest continues to thrive. His playing history and accomplishments are second to none. No one has ever done it before and most likely no one will ever do it again. In fact, to this very day Count Yogi is still considered to be the only perfect and consistent golfer (never to have been off his game) in the history of the world!!!

Harry M. Frankenberg A.K.A. Count Yogi vs. Bobby Jones

This story took place in 1929, one year before Bobby Jones won his historic "Grand Slam" and Bobby's game was about as sharp as it would ever be. George Dawson, the assistant to the president of Spalding Sports, Keith Spalding, was a believer and admirer of Harry M. Frankenberg—the young golf sensation out of

Chicago. Dawson's boss, was a Bobby Jones's admirer. George would eventually tell Keith about this young golfing phenom and how he had to see him play to appreciate his amazing talent. This intrigued Keith so much that he agreed to set up a golf match between young Harry and Bobby Jones the next time Bobby was in town for business. Spalding and Dawson would join the two, making it a foursome.

It wasn't long before Bobby found his way to Chicago—perhaps hastened by the fact that he, too, was intrigued and curious to see if young Harry was half as good as what he had heard. After brief introductions, they began their 18-hole match. Harry took the lead after the second hole and increased it as the match wore on. In the end, young Harry cruised to a fairly easy four stroke win over Jones who was in excellent form, shooting a 68. After the round, Bobby expressed his astonishment of Harry's poise and playing ability, saying that he played a game of grace, style and class of which he was unfamiliar. In fact, Jones went so far as to say that Frankenberg was the best he had ever seen. (I had always thought that Nicklaus was the first golfer who played a game of which Bobby was unfamiliar. I guess I was wrong.)

In those days, when an honorable man lost a match to an opponent who presented himself honorably and gentlemanly, it was customary for the loser to give one of his golf clubs to the victor as a token of respect. Thus, Bobby Jones expressed his admiration by giving Harry one of his clubs. Unfortunately, it's become a mystery as to which club it was and what happened to it. Other than that, we know everything about it.

Beating Bobby Jones had negative repercussions. Up until the day of the match, Harry had been receiving free Spalding Sports equipment such as golf balls, ping-pong balls and paddles (used for eye-hand coordination practice) and bowling shoes for his indoor golf school. It was quite apparent, though, that Harry's vanquishing of Bobby in that informal match infuriated Keith Spalding, as after that day, he cut Harry off from receiving any additional free Spalding merchandise—effectively, punishing Harry for playing too good and beating the great Bobby Jones. Dawson felt bad about Keith's irrational retaliation against Harry but was helpless to do anything about it. Didn't that stink!

Who transformed Ben Hogan's golf game and cured his hook?
Count Yogi

According to uncovered documents of conversations with Count Yogi, along with Chicago newspaper announcements and photos, Ben Hogan was first introduced to Yogi (the Great Frankenberg) in 1938. He began training with Yogi in the Winter/Spring (mostly indoors) of 1939-40. Yes, that is why his hooking problem went away and YES, because of Yogi's training he began to win!!!

Much of Hogan's discovery can be found in Yogi's first book; *"Revolutionary Golf Made Easy"* ©. This is the book that our #6 forgotten golfing legend, Tommy Armour, called the greatest book on golf ever written. There are only a handful of original copies left in existence; one is in the U.S.G.A. Library and another in the Count Yogi ® Golf archives. After being out of print and unavailable for over 70 years, there is now an electronic version available to the public at: http:// www.countyogi.com.

Hogan's benefactor, who introduced him to Count Yogi, was a wealthy Texan by the name of Marvin Leonard who owned a chain of department stores and built Colonial Country Club in 1936. Ironically, it's the same country club that would later become known as "Hogan's Alley." Ben caddied for Mr. Leonard as a youth at the Glen Garden Country Club. Marvin took a fond liking to Ben and eventually became a mentor, adopting him like a son and was instrumental in sending Ben to Yogi for help with his struggling game. So Hogan went to work with the "Great Frankenberg" out of Chicago, which back then was considered the "Golf Capital of The World"!!!

The fact is that Hogan's entire career began to dramatically improve and he started winning much more consistently after his training with Count Yogi concluded in 1940. Another piece of factual history is that, prior to 1940, Byron Nelson could beat Hogan most of the time, but after that everything changed. Byron played a heavy tournament schedule during the war years when Ben and many others were involved in military service. However, Nelson quickly retired at a young age about a year after Hogan and all the other great golfers returned home. Many believe that if Byron had not retired early, it would have been very unlikely that he would have ever dominated Hogan again like he did in their youthful years.

Count Yogi conquers Spain

This is a true story that was passed down by Horton Smith, the old-time golfing great who won the first and third Masters tournaments. He was a close friend of Yogi's up until Horton's death in 1963.

In the late 1940s (exact date uncertain), Yogi traveled to England to perform for the Royal Family and give lessons to Edward, Prince of Wales—the monarch who gave up his crown (but not his money) to marry a divorced American actress. Back in those days, Yogi would play the invitee's 18-hole course, which he had never seen before and then perform his show. In this case, like many times before, he broke the course record—winning over the gallery and the pro, as usual.

However, there was a wealthy Spaniard in the crowd who boasted, obnoxiously, about the extreme difficulty of his home course and that the course record of 66 had not been broken or matched in years. Then, in front of the crowd, he asked Yogi if he thought he could better that record.

It was obvious to Yogi and the gallery that this arrogant and envious man was trying to discredit Yogi. But not being one to ever back down from a challenge, Yogi announced to the man, "I accept your challenge." Then added, "Besides paying for all my expenses, what extra will you pay me for shooting a 65?" The man gave him a dollar figure. Then Yogi asked, "How about a 64?" Again he was given a higher dollar amount. Then Yogi asked, finally, "How much if I shoot a 63?" The man gave him a figure that was higher yet, but added in anger, "But if you don't shoot a 63, even if you shoot a 64 or 65, you get nothing!" To which Yogi replied with a big smile, "IT'S A DEAL!"

When Yogi arrived in Spain and found his way to that wealthy man's course, prior to teeing off, he took a blank scorecard and wrote in the score of 63. Then he proceeded to play the course with this fellow, and a large gallery following them. What score did Yogi shoot, in front of the crowd? A 63, of course!!

Count Yogi's legendary performances

This is not widely known among golfers of today, but in 1968 Byron Nelson was asked in an interview if he was impressed with Count Yogi's trick artistry show. He made the hurtful comment that Yogi was a fraud and that any good pro could perform those shots. When Yogi heard of it he asked Byron if he would come out of retirement and play him in an exhibition round and then perform his show with him. They were both similar in age (Yogi was a few years older), so it seemed like a very fair proposition. Unfortunately, Byron declined Yogi's challenge.

However, Billy Casper, who was the top golfer on the PGA Tour at the time, heard about it and accepted Yogi's challenge and offer to see if Yogi was, in fact, as good as he claimed to be. As the world now can see through documented film footage of that day, Billy Casper, the number one PGA golfer in the world, was made a believer by Yogi's superior shot making ability and became a Count Yogi fan. In fact, Casper remained a close friend of Yogi, until the day he died.

Yogi expressed his belief that Ben could have been even greater if he would have gone all the way with what Yogi wanted and instructed him to do. However, Ben was so pleased with his results that he stopped short of all the knowledge that was given to him but was eternally grateful for what Yogi had done for him. There is no doubt that when one closely examines and filters through the facts, dates, and evidence, without the influence and help from "the Master", Count Yogi, there would never had been a Ben Hogan, "legendary golfer". The history of Ben's serious golf problems and how they were fixed are very obscure and mostly unaddressed. We all know that Ben never claimed or stated that he did it on his own and knowing the fact that Ben was a major "recluse", no pro has ever dared to claim that he helped Hogan. No, the clouded historical truth is that Harry M. Frankenberg, aka Count Yogi fixed and helped set the path for Hogan's profound and successful career.

In the earlier days of golf and in the years since then, Harry "Montana" Frankenberg, aka Count Yogi, worked with and influenced countless other golfers. Following Yogi's instruction, many amateurs and professionals were able to realize their goals and fulfill their potential. Legendary golf names from all over the globe, except those who were jealous of Yogi, would listen closely to him when he talked.

In 1953 after witnessing one of Yogi's 7,000 + perfect shot shows performed in Hamilton, Canada, a young man in the gallery who witnessed the performance was so greatly impressed and influenced by the Count that he approached him afterwards with a barrage of eager questions. Yogi being the kind and patient person he was spent a few hours with him to answer all of his questions before packing up and heading to his next town and booking. The name of that young man was Moe Norman.

Without question, Count Yogi is one of the most copied and influential people in the history of the game. Yet in the world of golf today he has been lost with most people being completely unaware he and his contributions to the game ever existed. The late great President, John F. Kennedy when a Senator and taking lessons from Yogi told him; *"Yogi, you are the most exploited, un-exploited individual I have ever met!"* His ageless youthful method is nearly completely opposite of the way golf is instructed today which he felt was being taught "Backwards"!

It was written up in many articles in the late 1940s and early 1950s on how numerous pros, including Hogan, sought out Yogi to work out and practice with him while traveling through Los Angeles, Yogi 's newly adopted home (at that time). Yogi had opened up and operated a Golf Range and Training Center on Wilshire Boulevard where the Tishman Building stands today.

In later years, Yogi's good friend and astounding actor/entertainer Mickey Rooney had Yogi in scenes of the legendary wacky and zany movie; "It's A Mad, Mad, Mad, World!!!" Due to time and length restrictions, Yogi's and other cameo actors' appearances ended up on the cutting room floor. This is how the photos of the "Hindu" shots came about shortly after Yogi completed an 18-hole scoring exhibition at Fox Hills C.C. in Los Angeles. Yogi wore the costume to prove that clothing should never be an excuse for playing or scoring badly using his revolutionary system. Yogi ended up shooting a 64, wearing the Hindu costume.

Legendary sportswriter Jim Murray: "Yogi is the Undisputed Master of Golf, the master of the tee shot and the intentional slice! He can hit shots better than any pro I've ever seen."

Dean of sportswriters Grantland Rice: "Golf will roll along on its own merit. It does not need tournaments, Rose Bowl games or World Series, but teachers like Count Yogi to nurture the game to maturity."

Heavyweight Boxing Champion Mohammed Ali: "Yogi is like me, he's the greatest of all times!"

This photo is from a testimonial that was filmed in the late 1970's just prior to Ali fighting Leon Spinks in a rematch to win the heavyweight championship for the third time. It's believed that Yogi was the only athlete, other than himself, that the Champ ever called the greatest.

Tim Nicholls personally came to know the Count around 1962 at the tender age of 11. Tim had grown up with two of his children. From time to time when the Count would be passing through the Los Angeles area, Tim would visit with him. Tim didn't play golf or know much about the game then, but when he would see Yogi perform or play eighteen holes, he'd say to himself, "boy, what he can do with those golf balls."

As Tim grew, he not only got into the game, but learned to play it Yogi's way. He became like his adopted son and was personally mentored and taught by Yogi all of his intricate secrets of the art form. Tim was charged and has dedicated himself to keeping the Count Yogi method alive.

Count Yogi to this day will be remembered as the only world class Pro in the history of the game of golf to have never been off his game or ever needed a lesson from anyone. Just his Creator given, infallible mental routine and art form. Should not our honesty and intelligence to ourselves beckon to our common sense to learn and know what Yogi knew??

To learn more about this go online and visit https://www.countyogi.com the Count Yogi ® historical book site, and https://www.countyogigolf.com the Count Yogi ® Golf Co. Instruction/Training site.

Four most legendary PGA tournament wins

All four belong to Count Yogi's star pupil—Ben Hogan. He accomplished them with a battered body and pitiful putting—likely blamed on the left-eye injury he suffered in his car crash. Ben won six of his nine majors after the accident.

One of golf's most famous shots took place on the 18th fairway of Merion Golf Club in Pennsylvania. Only 16 months after a near-fatal car accident, Ben Hogan miraculously was in contention for a second U.S. Open title. On a foggy February evening in 1949 while Hogan was heading home from the PGA Tour's West Coast swing, a Greyhound bus collided with Hogan's Cadillac. Hogan flung himself in front of his wife, Valerie, but in the process suffered a crushing blow to his pelvis along with a broken collarbone and ankle. Hogan nearly died on the operating table. But nearly a year and hundreds of hours of rehabilitation later, Hogan returned to competition. He was far from healed at the 1950 U.S. Open. Underneath his trousers he was bandaged up like a mummy from waist to ankles. Every step he took was painful, yet Ben fought through the agony over 36 grueling holes on that final Saturday. (The U.S. Open in those days featured a 36-hole finale.) When Hogan reached the 72nd hole, he shared the lead with George Fazio and Lloyd Mangrum. A par on one of Merion's most challenging holes—an uphill par-4 measuring 458 yards—would get Hogan into an 18-hole playoff the next day. All golf historians know what happened next—Hogan's 1-iron approach shot found the green. The moment is etched in our memory. Hogan likely would have hit his 4-wood to the green, but he wasn't hitting that club well and he wasn't about to make a mistake that would put him out of the tournament. Thus, Hogan went ahead and hit the majestic 1-iron shot for which he would become forever famous. After two putts, Hogan ensured his spot in a playoff which he won the next day, by four strokes. Hogan would hit a 5-iron second shot into 18 during the playoff, having regained strength with a good night's sleep and perhaps more adrenaline. He was far more relaxed, having plenty of cushion with a four-stroke lead. Final scores were Hogan 69, Mangrum 73 and Fazio 75.

Hogan wins 1953 Masters with a tournament record 274

Ben made The Masters his first PGA Tour stop in 1953 and arrived two weeks early to get in plenty of practice in Augusta. Some who saw Hogan practice were calling him the favorite. But as tournament time rolled around, Lloyd Mangrum was getting most of the attention after firing a new course record of 10-under par-63, in a practice round. However, as Hogan would be quick to tell you, practice-round golf and tournament golf are two different animals. Hogan opened with rounds of 70-69, before shooting a third-round 66 that put him in the lead by four. Playing in the final round with Byron Nelson, Hogan fired a final round 69 for a 14-under par total and a five-stroke win that shattered the Masters by five. Afterwards, Ben called it his best 72-hole performance in tournament competition. As an added bonus, he clobbered Nelson by 23 shots, who had beaten him 11 years earlier in a stinging Masters playoff defeat.

Hogan wins 1953 U.S. Open for his fifth National Open title

In this photo, galleries follow Ben Hogan in 1953 Open at Oakmont, on his way to his fourth U.S. Open title by six strokes over Sam Snead. This gave Ben the second leg of the Triple Crown. Believe it or not, Hogan had to qualify for the national championship, even though he had won three of the previous five. After winning his fifth U.S. Open title, Hogan commented, "They played the Open at the wrong golf course." He was referring to the Pittsburgh Field Club where the qualifying was held. If Ben Hogan said they played on the wrong course, they played it on the wrong fricken course! Forcing Hogan to qualify was outrageous!

While this was Hogan's fourth official U.S. Open win, he also won the Hale America National Open in 1942 which is not counted as a U.S. Open win. Nevertheless, it was understood that due to World War II, this was merely a special name used for the U.S. Open that year. Hogan should be credited with a five U.S. Open wins.

Hogan wins 1954 British Open at Carnoustie on first try, after Masters and U.S. Open wins, to complete the Hogan slam

Ben Hogan's 1953 Open win will be viewed as one of the best Open achievements. Hogan, like every other golfer in the world, was well aware of the unique Grand Slam that amateur Bobby Jones accomplished in 1930, winning both the British Amateur and the British Open. In Hogan's case, his resume was lacking a British Open win and he needed to fill that void. Due to the measly purse offered by the British Open, first-place prize money wasn't enough to cover travel and lodging expenses for Americans who entered the tournament. Thus, very few American golfers entered since 1930.

Perhaps the bigger concern for Hogan was the Open was being held at Carnoustie, a course notoriously windy and tough on a golfer's body—precisely what Ben did not need on his battered body.

But believing his career would be incomplete without a British Open win, he made the trip to Scotland in late June. Despite his Masters and U.S. Open victories, British rules required him to play two qualifying rounds on June 29 and 30 before the tournament began. He turned in a decent 145, but it didn't seem so hot compared to the 136 shot by defending champion Bobby Locke. Nevertheless, Hogan was comfortably within the 154 cut.

This was a time when the British Open and PGA Championship stupidly were held virtually simultaneously. Thus, it was impossible to play in all four majors. On top of that, the most important tournament in all of Europe was held on Wednesday, Thursday and Friday—so the course could be available for members on the weekend. Worst of all for Hogan, it concluded with a grueling 36-hole finale. Organizers of golf's major championships in Britain and the U.S. were morons back in those days.

In spite of everything, Hogan finished the Open with an excellent final round of 68 for a 72-hole total of 282, the second lowest score in the tournament's history. Hogan started the day, on Friday, two strokes behind Dai Rees and Eric Brown. However, he managed to shoot rounds of 70-68 to come from behind and win the tournament by four shots, despite his substantial physical handicaps and mediocre putting.

The Scottish crowds begrudgingly came to acquire deep admiration for Hogan—even though he ridiculed the course conditions upon his arrival, and commented that he had a lawn mower back in in Texas that he was willing to loan them.

In the early going, British announcers insinuated Hogan was *fortunate* to be hitting every fairway and green during the first two rounds. However, when he continued his masterful ball-striking exhibition into the fourth round, they were forced to admit that Hogan was simply a great golfer. The crowds went on to affectionately nickname him the "Wee Ice Mon" as the 5-foot 7-inch 145-pound Hogan conquered Carnoustie. His methodical and exacting approach led the sixth hole at Carnoustie to be known as "Hogan's Alley."

That sixth hole is a par-5 with a split fairway. The safer play is to go up the wider right side, but the line that results in a better approach is to play to the narrower left side, which is lined with bunkers on one side and out of bounds on the other. Hogan chose the gutsier approach—down the left fairway every round—and hit the fairway all four times. And by Hogan's Alley that hole will be known forevermore.

Count Yogi and Bobby Locke encounter

None of these four historic major championship victories by Hogan would have been possible without the coaching from Count Yogi. Although the great Count Yogi was blackballed out of an opportunity to participate in PGA Tour events, he left an indelible mark on PGA Tour history through the success of Ben Hogan, Yogi's most famous student.

Tim Nicholls, manager of Count Yogi Golf Co., tells the story when in 1947, in Miami, Bobby Locke had come to the U.S. after trouncing Sam Snead 12 to 4 in the $15,000 winner-take-all challenge match series in South Africa. At a gala event at a Miami hotel, attended by top people in the golf scene, Locke was acting rather pompous about his easy defeat over Snead. A fellow at the party, who was familiar with Yogi, said to Locke, "There's one guy in the room here this evening who is better than any of the PGA Tour pros and, in fact, he could even beat you." Locke stared at the guy annoyingly and asked him who his incredible golfer was and that he would like to meet this fellow. The guy pointed out Yogi.

Locke introduced himself and Yogi said, "Yes, I know who you are." "I hear you're a pretty good golfer, maybe even better than any of the PGA Tour pros," said Locke. "Yes, that's true," said Yogi. "I recently gave Sam Snead a good shellacking in a challenge match series where I beat him 12 to 4," says Locke. "Yes, I have heard," replies Yogi. "If I raise the prize money do you want to challenge me?" asks Locke. "Absolutely! How much?" "I'm thinking $15,000." "Make it $30,000." "Thirty-thousand dollars? I played Sam Sneed for $15,000!" "Well, I'm not Sam Snead." "Wait here a minute, let me go over and talk to my agent."

Bobby walked over to his agent and said, "Good news, I think I just found a pigeon we can make some big money off of. This guy wants to take me on in a $30,000 challenge match, winner-take-all." To which his agent asked, "Who is this pigeon you're referring to?" Locke pointed over to Count Yogi, of whom his agent was well familiar and he replied, "No, you don't want to play against him. That's the great 'Frankenberg' out of Chicago. He's so good they won't even let him on the PGA Tour because he'd beat everybody. Some players are so superstitious that they believe he uses magic!" "That sounds ridiculous. Nobody's that good." To which his agent replied, "If that's the case, then his name IS NOBODY. Believe me, from everything I've heard about him, you definitely don't want to play that guy. He's the guy that all of the top pros go to for help because he's better than everyone else. There are too many other guys on the PGA Tour who you can easily beat. Don't mess around with Count Yogi. Even if you did beat him, which I don't believe you can, what would it gain you since many know not of him? But if he beats you, your name and recent accomplishments are suddenly and greatly diminished while his reputation gets a big boost! No, it's bad business. We're staying away from this guy."

As you may have guessed, the winner-take-all challenge match between Locke and Yogi never took place. However, this was no surprise to Yogi as he became known as the guy who was, virtually, unbeatable. Thus, none of the top players wanted to go up against him and embarrass themselves. Fortunately, for them, Yogi enjoyed teaching and entertaining and the pros were happy to have him in that capacity so that they wouldn't have to deal with him in tournament competition.

Ironically, Count Yogi was the first great golfer to be blackballed by the PGA Tour, in the 1930s, and Bobby Locke, who employed a similar elliptical swing style and putting style as Yogi's, was the second player to be blackballed, in the 1940s.

Count Yogi's powerful presence

Tim shared one other interesting Count Yogi story with me which involved a personal encounter with a golfer by the name of Jack Nicklaus. The year was 1981 and Tim and Yogi were attending the opening round of the Los Angeles Open at Riviera Country Club. Tim was excited when he saw Jack heading from the 9th green to the 10th tee, so he asked Yogi if he could watch him tee off and Yogi said "Okay".

Nicklaus, like all of the touring pros of his era, had heard the old stories of Yogi's legendary scoring feats and miracle show performances along with the discrimination he had endured. Tim showed me an old faded photo from the early 1960s of Jack and Yogi shaking hands. We're guessing that's when they met for the first time.

Getting back to the story, the incident that took place was something I found difficult to imagine. Jack was about to tee off on the 10th hole when he caught a glimpse of Yogi standing nearby, in the gallery. Inexplicably, Jack (the defending Masters Champion) became nervous and befuddled, realizing that Yogi was watching him hit his tee shot—even though Yogi was a 72-year-old man at the time. As Jack completed his back swing, he proceeded to come unglued—hitting a foot behind the ball with his driver, taking a massive divot and dribbling the ball off the tee!! That's something that would have been a bit shocking to witness at the state amateur level, let alone a PGA Tour event from the most accomplished Tour player of all time. Suffice to say, Tim was left dumbfounded.

To this day, he has been unable to figure out why Jack fell apart so horrifically on that particular shot with a driver and perfect teed up lie. Was it because of the shame and guilt he felt about the persecution and unfair treatment Yogi had been subjected to by the PGA Tour? Or was it just plain awe of Yogi's reputation and presence? Perhaps a little of both. There were numerous articles written between the 1930s and 1960s, from various journalists who commented that all the pros became nervous while in the presence of Yogi. Putting yourself in Jack's shoes, imagine everyone in the world calling you the greatest. Yet, in your heart and mind, you're familiar with but never competed against the man who was the true greatest golfer of all time who most people are unfamiliar with.

In regard to Nicklaus, he's a superstar deserving of great accolades and shouldn't be judged by one bad golf swing in tournament competition. More than anything, this story reveals the power of Yogi's presence, even as an old man. I'm guessing that if someone as important as President Reagan had been there watching him, Jack would have calmly nailed a 300-yard drive down the middle of the fairway. But Yogi watching him, that's a different story.

Count Yogi's Incredible scoring feats

- In 1932, he recorded seven birdies in succession, shooting a 64 at Golfmoor Country Club, breaking Walter Hagen's course record.
- In 1933, he played a 645-yard par-6 hole in three strokes for an albatross and recorded a 59 on a par-74 course.
- In 1934, as previously mentioned, he shot 26-29 for a 55 at Bunker Hill Golf Course, a regulation course, winning the Chicago Golf Championship.
- In 1938, he shot a 64 at Timber Trails to win a Visking event.
- In 1939, he reeled off eight birdies and two eagles in succession to a 58 at Paw Paw Lakes Links in Michigan.
- Also in 1939, he shot a 63 at Elmhurst Country Club to win the National Furniture Championship.
- Again in 1939, he shot a 65 at the Westward Ho! Country Club to win the National Tool and Die Open.
- In 1941, he reeled off seven birdies in a row for a world tournament record (held for 18 years) in the Chicago Open at Elmhurst Country Club, which was won by Ben Hogan.
- In 1940, he averaged 67.7 per round for 203 rounds of 18-hole golf—playing both right and left-handed.
- In 1944, he shot a 64 while playing with Jerry Zalkind at Glenbard Country Club in Chicago on March 31. This was his first round of golf on this par-72 layout and he broke the course record held by George Dawson—the great amateur vice president of A. G. Spaulding.
- During a single day in 1944, he played seven 18-hole rounds of golf at Bunker Hill Golf Course, from 7 a.m. to 9 p.m., while recording consistently low scores of 69, 66, 67, 66, 67, 68 and 67. He accomplished this walking quickly and using his "infallible mental routine." This feat required tremendous physical conditioning to walk 35-40 miles in one day, while hitting a total of 470 golf shots—never miss-hitting a single shot!
- In 1948, he played 18 holes in 57 minutes, scoring a 69 at the Mid-City Golf Course, Chicago. This was the fastest round ever played while walking.

- Also in 1948, he shot a course record 63 (31-32) at Bel Air Country Club in Los Angeles.
- In 1949, he shot a 65 (34-31) on a par-73 layout, winning Metro Goldwyn Mayer's Annual Open.
- Also in 1949, he shot a 67 (31-36) at Western Avenue Golf Course in Los Angeles to win a Universal International event, wearing a Hindu suit.
- Again in 1949, he recorded seven wins and two runner-up finishes in Pro-Am events.
- In 1952, he shot a 63 (31-32) on par-72 Grossinger Golf Club in New York—breaking the records held by Sam Snead, Lew Worsham and Lloyd Mangrum.
- He played 18 holes with only 14 putts, scoring 29-29-58 on par-72 Wilson Golf Course in Griffith Park at the 1951 Los Angeles Open.
- In his career, he broke 60 (for 18-holes) four times—shooting scores of 55, 57, 58 and 59.
- He shot 59 to win the best ball title, playing without a partner, at Greenview Country Club in Chicago.
- He scored an albatross on a 550-yard par-5 hole in Corpus Christi, Texas—smashing his drive 453 yards and holing-out his second shot with a wedge.
- He shot par or under in 267 of 273 successive exhibition shows.
- During his career he recorded drives of 453, 450, 435 and 425 yards.
- He recorded 55 hole-in-ones—nine of them on par-4 holes and two in succession, 187 and 347 yards, with one 416-yard hole-in-one.
- He shot 69 or under nearly every round of his professional career.

These incredibly amazing scoring feats are a testament to the phenomenal golfing talent that Count Yogi possessed and make a strong argument in support of his induction into the World Golf Hall of Fame. Undoubtedly, if Yogi had been a regular PGA Tour member, he could have easily won a dozen majors, if not twice that many.

It is the opinion of this author that a motion picture about Count Yogi should be made for the benefit of the world.

CHAPTER 14

ED "PORKY" OLIVER

1940 U.S. Open
Legendary pro golf
disqualifications
and other blunders

P orky Oliver shot a 71 in the final round of the 1940 U.S. Open, which put him in a three-way tie for the lead with Gene Sarazan and Lawson Little. But rainy weather was on its way, so old Porky's group teed off before their scheduled time, and the official starter was not on the ball.

Despite protests from Sarazen and Little, who thought he should be included in the playoff, tournament officials disqualified Porky. The 5-foot 9-inch, 240-pound Oliver became known for coming very close on numerous occasions but unable to win a major—yet not letting it bother him. Sadly, he died at 46.

It's bad enough they called him Porky, but they also had to punish him for arriving early for his tee time and teeing off when the group ahead was out of range. Isn't that what starters are supposed to encourage?

Porky's revenge?

You've heard of Porky's Revenge, right? Here's Porky being congratulated by Bobby Jones, with Ben Hogan. Did you forget Porky's Masters victory? Why else would this Delaware sports legend be wearing a Masters Green Jacket? Looking at the photo, I can't help but notice Porky has a cigarette in his hand. Could that have something to do with why he died so young—just eight years after this photo was taken?

Lumpy's resemblance to Porky

Porky reminds me, eerily, of a less acclaimed professional golfer out of Minnesota by the name of Tim Herron and affectionately known as Lumpy. As of this writing, Tim is 44 years old, roughly the same height and weight as Porky was and still alive—but he's not 46 yet.

To Tim's credit, he's managed four PGA Tour wins and over $18 million in career earnings—making him, easily, the second most accomplished pro golfer in Minnesota history. As recently as 2006, he was in the top 50 of the World Golf Rankings. However, he has since lost his tour card and fallen to number 717. I wonder what could have caused that?

Instead of working out, Tim prefers to sit on his couch eating munchies and watching a video of someone else working out. Worst of all, he expects to achieve the same results as Jane Fonda. When I tried coaxing Lumpy into trying the ultimate fitness routine that I developed, he said he would probably have a heart attack after 30 seconds. However, I was willing to bet Tim was wrong and that it would take a full minute before he went into cardiac arrest.

It's not like losing 70 pounds is going to kill Tim. Not losing the weight could do that. On the other hand, I could be wrong and Tim may have nothing to worry about. Lumpy also reminds me of comedians John Candy and Chris Farley. They must be in their 50s and 60s by now. They're both still alive and well, right?

Tim is a great guy with a terrific sense of humor and it would be a terrible shame for his family, friends and the golf world to lose him at an early age. He just needs motivation to commit to a serious weight loss program. I'm here to help, Tim, if you need me. Also, don't forget that I pulled for you in all of your PGA Tour wins (except for your 1999 Bay Hill playoff defeat of Tom Lehman). I still haven't forgiven you for that.

Jackie Pung, 1957 U.S. Women's Open

A half hour after Jackie Pung walked off Winged Foot's 18th green, the apparent Women's U.S. Open winner, a USGA official announced that she was disqualified for reporting an incorrect score on the fourth hole on her final round. It felt like an important person had suddenly died, or the official was playing a cruel joke on everyone. It was incomprehensible something so unfair could happen to this talented Hawaiian woman.

Jackie had handed in the correct total for her final round— a 72. Her card did, however, show a 5 and not the 6 she had taken on the fourth. But her addition took into account that it was actually a 6, and her total was correct. The shocking news filled everyone with anger, grief and compassion over this brutal ruling based on such a minor technicality.

The members of Winged Foot spontaneously undertook a collection for Jackie and that very evening raised more than $2,000 for her—a nice gesture, but not as nice as being the winner and handed the U.S. Open trophy.

The trophy was presented to the official winner, Betsy Rawls, and she was quick to accept it which was a mistake. She should have handed the trophy to Jackie, saying, "This trophy belongs to you. You're the only deserving winner here." Jackie would have appreciated that and Betsy Rawls would have been remembered as the classiest woman in the history of the Ladies PGA Tour— instead of a woman who won eight fricken majors. Heavens to Betsy, you blew that one.

You're probably thinking that by trophy presentation time, Betsy's name was already engraved into the trophy. But before it was engraved, Betsy could have insisted that it not be done.

Upon hearing the terrible news, Jackie broke down and left the club with her 15-year-old daughter. She managed to calm herself and return, amazingly stoic about the whole experience. "Winning the Open is the greatest thing in golf," she began her remarks at the presentation ceremonies. "I have come close before. This time I thought I'd won. But I didn't. Golf is played by rules, and I broke a rule. I've learned a lesson. And I have two broad shoulders...." What a courageous woman!

Nevertheless, both Gary and I would have been clever enough to easily dispute that ridiculous disqualification and be quickly reinstated as the U.S. Open champion. All we would had to have done is say that the 5 on the scorecard looked awfully close to a 6 (which a five does). Then we would have asked to take a look at the scorecard again. Upon examining the card in front of the entire crowd (with microphone in hand) we would say, "That certainly looks like 6 to me. With a 6 on that hole, what does that give me for an 18-hole score?" (72) "Isn't that what I signed for?" (Yes, it is) "Then what's the problem, other than the fact that you seem to have a hard time telling a 6 from a 5??"

If Jackie had followed that script, the rules official would have been forced to accept that logical explanation, reinstate Jackie as the winner and apologize profusely for the stupid mistake on his part.

I wish I could have been at Winged Foot to save the day for poor Jackie.

Doug Sanders, 1966 Pensacola Open

Sanders was tearing up the course the first 36 holes of the 1966 Pensacola Open, shooting rounds of 63 and 67. Sanders, the defending champion, opened up a four-stroke lead at that point. When is a lead of four shots (or even 20 shots) not good enough? Any kind of lead is never enough if a player forgets to sign his scorecard.

He got so busy signing autographs from adoring fans that he forgot to sign his name when it mattered the most, before leaving the course. He lost the $10,000 first-prize money that wound up going to Gay Brewer, and $25,000 in bonuses from his sponsors. You'd think he would have known better, having won the Pensacola Open two previous times, along with 14 other PGA Tour events. When Doug's not kicking himself over throwing away a British Open victory in 1970, he's probably beating himself up over this stupid Pensacola Open blunder.

Roberto De Vicenzo, 1968 Masters

In 1968, Roberto De Vicenzo learned the hard way that he couldn't trust the scores written down for him by his playing partner. Roberto missed a playoff for the coveted Green Jacket by one stroke due that simple blunder. At first it appeared that he had tied Bob Goalby and the two would meet in an 18-hole Monday playoff, but De Vicenzo (the reigning British Open champion) returned an incorrect scorecard showing a par-4 on the 17th hole, instead of a 3, where he birdied it with an easy 2-foot putt.

Roberto was penalized due to a scoring error made by his playing partner Tommy Aaron—the idiot who erroneously marked the 4, on a hole where Roberto had a kick-in birdie. Unfortunately, De Vicenzo failed to catch the mistake before signing the scorecard. USGA rules stated that the higher written score signed by a golfer on his card must stand.

Golf pro Jimmy Demaret rallied for Roberto, saying, "Twenty-five million people witnessed De Vicenzo making birdie on the 17th hole and that would have held up in a court of law." However, it didn't hold up in Bobby Jones's court; he always abided strictly to USGA rules. Although Roberto wasn't disqualified, he did miss out on a chance at immortality and a lot of money. Do you remember what De Vicenzo said afterward, to become one of the most famous quotes in the history of pro golf?

Ironically, De Vicenzo believed he became more popular and famous for losing the Masters through his scorecard blunder than he would have if he'd won the tournament. I would agree. Tommy Aaron, for example, is a Masters champion and people have forgotten about him. But we'll always sympathize with De Vicenzo. Who could forget the man who said, "What a stupid I am!" I certainly won't.

There's a woman in the De Vicenzo photo with her hand on his shoulder, consoling him, saying, "Cheer up Roberto. You can get 'em next year." Roberto reportedly replied to the woman in Spanish. I don't know what Roberto said to her. Her comment was uninformed—as if the opportunity to win the Masters comes along every year. But Roberto probably responded to her kindly, appreciating her optimism. He was a really sweet guy. That's why he was well loved and everybody felt sorry for him—with the possible exception of Bob Goalby.

Speaking of Goalby, I don't care what Jay Haas says about him. I think he's a great guy. Dave Hill, in his book *Teed Off*, described Bob Goalby as the nicest and most courteous golfer on the PGA Tour.

I would like to think other golfers view me as being that much of a gentleman, but that may be asking too much.

Paul Azinger, 1991 Doral Ryder, from ecstacy to agony

During the opening round of the 1991 Doral Open, Paul Azinger's approach shot on the 18th hole finished on the edge of the water hazard, fronting the green. Since the ball was only partly submerged, he waded in the water to give the ball a whack. He stepped on a small rock or coral and dislodged it. If you step on a rock in the water, it's probably going to move. Paul managed to play the shot successfully and escape with a bogey for a 69—not bad.

The following day he did even better, shooting a 65. This put Azinger within just a stroke of the lead, heading into the weekend—sweet! But not so fast. A TV viewer waited a day before calling in to rat out Azinger for a rules violation.

Rules official Mike Shea admitted he was too stupid to realize a rules violation was committed. Shea couldn't claim that he *didn't* witness the infraction—that would have been hard to do unless he was out to lunch. As I recall, Azinger was in the final group of the day and all eyes were on him.

The following day, Azinger argued that the violation was unintentional. But the rules of golf don't give a damn about intent and clearly state that the movement of a loose impediment in a hazard constitutes a two-stroke penalty (Rule 13-4c). Since he'd already signed Thursday's card, Shea went ahead and disqualified Azinger. Once again it was a guy on his couch who ratted—this time for something that Mike Shea should have noticed.

I remember the incident unfolding on TV and wondering why no penalty was called. But it was Shea's responsibility to call the penalty at the time of the violation—not the following day, along with a disqualification from the tournament. A golfer can live, begrudgingly, with a two-stroke penalty. But he can't live with a disqualification after shooting a great fricken round of golf!

The bigger rat was Mike Shea, who was not simply a rules official, but the tournament director! The PGA Tour finds a guy who's incapable of calling an obvious penalty and they make him tournament director? Not to be too hard on Shea, but was the tour practicing some idiotic system that rewarded incompetence?

There was an off-course incident involving Mike Shea around the same time which was cause to question his intelligence. I happened to be at a dinner party, which Mike also attended, when one of the guests started choking on a piece of meat. Mike rushed over to the guy, stood him up, pulled his pants down and licked his butt! I couldn't believe my eyes! I yelled over to Mike, "What in the hell are you doing?" Mike replied, "I'm doing the hind-lick maneuver, *stupid*!"

Craig "The Walrus" Stadler, 1987 San Diego Open

The Walrus thought he finished second at the 1987 San Diego Open. Then, a day later, he found out he had broken Rule 13-3 on the 14th hole. His ball landed in a muddy area next to a tree on that hole, and Stadler had to get down on his knees to hit the shot. But being the neat freak he was, Craig thought it was a good idea to throw a towel down to avoid getting his trousers dirty. But kneeling on a towel was considered "building a stance"—a rules violation.

Tournament officials should have recognized Stadler's violation—it was broadcast on national TV. But once again a TV viewer waited until the next day to rat Craig out, assuring his disqualification. Again the bigger rat was the rules official on the scene who missed it. He didn't call anything on Stadler at the time of the violation, but had no qualms about disqualifying Craig after the viewer called in.

I never found out who the rules official was. Please don't tell me it was Mike Shea again! The infraction cost the Walrus $37,000 in prize money. The good news is that Craig saved a couple bucks on his dry cleaning bill.

Greg Norman, 1990 Palm Meadows Cup

Entering the third round, a battle of two stars was about to unfold. Greg Norman had a one-shot lead over Curtis Strange. However, prior to teeing off, Greg made the determination that he had taken an improper ball drop from a water hazard during the first round. Norman disqualified himself, losing a chance at the first-place check of $160,000.

Here again, Gary would have been way too smart to concern himself with an insignificant incident, such as the correctness of a ball drop, that took place two days prior—especially when the drop would had to have been approved by his playing partners. Instead, Player would have been singularly focused on his third round strategy with the mindset of increasing his tournament lead.

Nick Price & Nick Faldo, 1992 Million Dollar Challenge

The disqualifications of these two Hall-of-Famers took a couple of the biggest stars out of the event—the first to offer a million dollars to the winner. The first disqualification came in the third round when Nick Faldo was disqualified for signing an incorrect scorecard. At the time, he was six shots behind the third-round leader and was awarded last-place money of $105,000. He still had a decent payday for someone who was six strokes out of the lead. Plus, he wound up only "working" three days.

The other disqualification happened to Nick Price, who was tied for the lead with David Frost. During the round, Price hit a drive into the fairway and his caddie moved an advertising board which was 25 yards ahead of Price's ball. However, the sign was deemed to be an immovable obstruction, so Price should have taken a free drop, as it clearly states in Rule 24-2 (b) i). He didn't know that, and after his round he signed (what turned out to be) an incorrect scorecard.

Even though tournament officials told Price that he could change the card, he rejected the offer out of foolish pride and left the premises, disqualifying himself. Price also received a check for a last-place finish. Nick Price, you too were a stupid! For crying out loud, this tournament took place at Gary Player Country Club—with Gary present! Gary would have advised you to *never* turn down a favorable ruling from a rules official.

Being tied for the lead with only one round to play, the disqualification could have cost him as much as $895,000—more than some people make in an entire year. Having said that, tongue in cheek, I would love to receive $105,000 for finishing last in a golf tournament. I'm pretty sure I could accomplish that feat without a lot of practice.

Nick Faldo, again, 1994 Alfred Dunhill Masters

Is it possible to lose a golf tournament you're leading by six shots with just seven holes left to play? Faldo proved it can be done.

Faldo was in this spot when some killjoy ratted him out for removing a piece of coral from behind his ball in a bunker. On the European Tour it was legal to do that. However this tournament, in Bali, Indonesia, was governed by the Australasian Tour in which it's illegal. Since Faldo had signed an incorrect scorecard following his third round, he was disqualified from the tournament, losing the first-place check of just over $100,000.

But that's small change for a guy as wealthy as Faldo, especially after *A Swing For Life* just sold its billionth copy. Nick is a friend of mine and he's a monster Steven Seagal fan. Believe it or not, he has watched the movie

Marked For Death at least a hundred times. Nevertheless, I'm glad I talked him out of going with the original title he planned for his book which was *A Swing For Death*.

Isao Aoki in the 1994 Doug Sanders Celebrity Classic

Halfway through the first round of this tournament, Aoki hit an approach shot that wound up buried in a bunker. After searching for five minutes, he declared the ball unplayable (in Japanese) and followed the rules by taking a drop and an extra stroke. However, by this time the bunker was loaded with footprints from their thorough search. So, they did the logical thing and raked the bunker so that Isao wouldn't have to play his next shot out of a footprint they had created in their search. That seems totally reasonable to me.

But here's another instance when the rules of golf really stink. It's illegal under any circumstances to rake a bunker before playing a shot out of it—even if you have a legitimate reason. No one on the scene noticed that Aoki had broken the rule. But he too was ratted out the following day by some couch potato—getting Aoki disqualified.

Aoki made it into the World Golf Hall of Fame with impressive credentials—one PGA Tour win, which was pure luck, and zero majors. My question is this: Did Aoki pay off the induction committee?? He's such a sneaky devil, they probably thought he was paying them off in dollars, but instead he paid them in yen.

Bob Murphy & Mike Joyce, 1995 Burnet Senior Classic—
a complicated situation with not one but two unnecessary
disqualifications

"Nice guys finish last" and sometimes they get disqualified—particularly if they're not very bright. After a weather delay at the 1995 Burnet Senior Classic, Bob Murphy returned to the fairway and put his ball down. While he waited for play to resume, he took a few playful practice putts. Later, he would call it "doodling to kill time."

Murphy's playing partner, Mike Joyce, asked a tournament official if such actions were against the rules and found out they were. Golfers are not allowed to practice on the competition course on the day of the tournament. But Joyce didn't report Murphy, because he didn't think what Bob was doing was really "practicing." After all, he was on the fairway, not the green. How could taking putts on a fairway help your game?

Nevertheless, two days later, Joyce told Murphy about the rule, just so he would know enough not to do it again in the brief future Murphy had left in competitive golf. However, Murphy insisted on doing the honorable, but stupid, thing and disqualified himself. Unfortunately, not ratting on someone who violated the rules is also, idiotically, a rules violation. Thoughtfully, the officials disqualified Joyce as well.

I think Joyce easily could have saved himself. Because the so-called practice happened during a rain delay, he could have said he wasn't watching Murphy very closely and couldn't be certain that Murphy violated the rule. The rules of golf certainly do not require someone to accuse their playing partner of a violation of which he may not have been guilty.

Gary Player, the old penalty-avoiding master, would have been clever enough to use that excuse to save himself from disqualification. All I can say is, what a stupid Mike Joyce was!

And Bob Murphy was even more stupid. If he had consulted Gary, he would have advised Bob to do the smart thing, and thank Joyce for the heads up, assuring him he would never make that silly mistake again.

Jeff Sluman, 1996 Bay Hill Invitational

Jeff Sluman was only two shots back of the leaders at this invitational after two rounds. But that night, going through the first two rounds in his head while lying in bed, he realized that he may have taken an illegal drop after hitting into a pond in the second round. The following day he returned to the scene and determined that he did indeed take an illegal drop— he inadvertently dropped the ball closer to the hole. Being far too honest, he reported the minor violation to get disqualified. Brilliant move, Jeff.

When you're lying in bed, do what I do—forget about everything and go to sleep. Or try a Kenny Perry and pretend you didn't notice your violation (see Chapter 15).

Greg Norman again, 1996 Cannon Greater Hartford Open

Norman, the defending champion, made the stupid decision to disqualify himself from this event (after the second round) for using golf balls that he determined to be "technically illegal." Idiotically, he made that determination despite claiming "The ball I used was legal and approved by the USGA." The, nearly undiscernible, problem involved the stamping on the Maxfli balls Greg was using that week. It should have read "XS-90." But his balls were stamped "XS-9" and for the lack of a zero Norman DQ'd himself, believing it was the honorable thing to do.

Gary, on the other hand, would have been way too smart to suffer disqualification had he been in the same situation. He would have (wisely) kept quiet about the silly lack of a zero on his ball, realizing that it's totally insane for a golf ball to be legal and USGA approved yet still be illegal. Of course, Player won nine majors and Norman won two. That sounds about right because Gary is probably more than four times smarter than Greg.

P.H. Horgan, 1996 Shreveport Open

P.H. Horgan III, playing some of the best golf of his life, tied for first in this Hogan Tour event. While he was waiting for the final groups to finish before the playoff with Tim Loustalot,

Horgan made the moronic decision to inform the tournament director of a possible rules violation on his part from the day before. On the green he accidentally dropped his ball on top of his ball marker and caused the marker to move before replacing it. Horgan's playing partners all concurred no infraction needed to be assessed.

Horgan's failure to let it to be forgotten not only knocked him out of the playoff but it disqualified him for violating Rule 20-1/5.5, which requires that he should have assessed himself a one-stroke penalty for causing his ball marker to move. Loustalot made off like a bandit, winning without a playoff and Horgan lost a lot.

He could have found the answer to this rules question in his rulebook and then be careful not to make a blunder like that again. Horgan had no reason to mention the incident to the tournament director, of all people.

I think it's idiotic to penalize a player for accidentally dropping a golf ball that he marked and is not in play, and happens to land on his ball marker, causing it to move. This rule should have been changed decades ago—but it's incredibly rare for that sort of thing to happen. Thus, who's going to complain about it?

Horgan managed to graduate from the Hogan Tour that year to the PGA Tour in which he went on to win absolutely nothing. Horgan's career U.S. Open record, from 1987 to 1997, was particularly impressive with zero cuts made.

It's a shame that Horgan, eligible for the 50-and-older circuit in 2010, didn't make it to the Champions Tour. I'm guessing he couldn't figure out where the qualifying was being held. He did finally make it to the Champion Tour's Q-School location in the fall of 2011 and went on to finish 70th on the money list with $153,800 in earnings in 2012. After which, he was rarely heard from again. I don't wish to be overly hard on old P.H., as I understand he's a hell of a nice guy—but that's his problem.

Davis Love, 1997 Players Championship

On the 71st hole of the tournament, Davis Love III inadvertently hit his ball on the putting green with a practice stroke. He did not replace the ball, two-putted from there, and scored himself as having a bogey 4. However, he should have replaced his ball to the original spot before continuing to putt. Failure to do so is a one-stroke penalty, and thus his score for the hole was actually a double-bogey 5.

This was another instance when officials were sleeping on the job as more than 100 million viewers at home watched it happen, as plain as day—me included. Once again the officials were schooled by a phone call from a TV viewer. As usual, they waited until Love signed his scorecard to inform him of the violation—ensuring he would suffer disqualification instead of finishing tied for 17th. The mistake cost Love $105,000 and Ryder Cup points.

Love should have returned the ball to the original position and I was surprised he didn't know that. But I didn't want to be the guy ratting him out. In hindsight, I wish I had called—that may have saved him from disqualification. But why the hell does saving the golf world rest on my shoulders?

Lee Janzen, 1998 World Series of Golf

It's unlikely Lee Janzen will forget his 34th birthday. After he arrived at Firestone Country Club for the second round of the World Series of Golf, he was promptly escorted into a meeting with rules officials who informed him he was disqualified.

Ratted out by a TV viewer who was watching Janzen from his couch, tournament officials watched a video of Janzen's first-round birdie putt on the par-4 17th hole. It was a putt that stopped right on the edge of the hole with part of the ball hanging over the lip of the cup—seemingly defying gravity. After at least 20 seconds, the ball finally dropped.

But that was five seconds too long and Janzen should have added a stroke to his score. Instead, Janzen signed for a 3. His birthday present was disqualification from a big tournament.

Roe, Parnevik disqualified from the 2003 British Open

Mark Roe and Jesper Parnevik were disqualified from the British Open in 2003 after failing to exchange scorecards at the first hole and signing the wrong scores. "What can you do?" Roe said. "I've just played one of the greatest rounds of my life and I can't play tomorrow." Roe finished with a 4-under 67 at Royal St George's that left him three shots off the lead.

Parnevik was at 81 to put him at 15 over. "I don't think it's fair," Parnevik said. "It's the dumbest rule I have ever heard of." They discovered the blunder at the end of the round, officials said. "It's a quite comical error," Roe said. "We didn't exchange on the first tee, so I marked my scores on my card and Jesper marked his scores on his card. After the round I checked it three times, but unfortunately we are disqualified." Parnevik said the two players checked their scores with the scorers and two Royal & Ancient officials initially said they were OK. Then they discovered they had been disqualified.

"How stupid is that?" Parnevik said. "We checked our scores with the scorers. We had two officials checking. I can't believe in the 10 minutes we were in there, they didn't catch it." Parnevik felt sorry for Roe. "He probably would have been leading the tournament after today," the Swede said.

Officials said if the players and scorers had discovered the mistake inside the scorers' hut, the problem could have been solved. Peter Dawson, secretary of the rule-making Royal & Ancient Club, said the organizers accepted the blame. "It's one of the great tragedies of championship golf," he said. "Our checking procedures have clearly failed and we take the blame for that, but not the responsibility. We feel very bad about this. We like to think we have procedures in place to prevent that from happening." But, obviously, they didn't.

That being the case, Dawson, due to negligence, should have provided financial settlements to Parnevik and especially Roe. Dawson took the blame for this nasty incident but not the responsibility for it!

Poor Mark Roe. He shoots the greatest round of his life, giving himself a great chance of winning the British Open, and signs a correct scorecard. Yet, he gets disqualified, even after the British Open officials tell him that his scores were recorded properly. How is that possible?

Spaniard Borja Etchart and Norwegian, Eirik Tage Johansen— involved in ball marking incident in the 2010 Open de Andalucia

Johansen learned the hard way that it's not a good idea to overlook multiple ball marking breaches by the player whose score you're keeping. Doing so resulted in disqualification for both Etchart and Johansen from the £896,000 European Tour event. In Etchart's case, he learned the meaning of the word blindsided (or *lado oculto*).

Rules Decision 33-7/9 explains why; "The responsibility for knowing the Rules lies with all players. In stroke play, the player and his marker have an explicit responsibility for the correctness of the player's score card."

The 21-year-old Spaniard was playing in just his third European Tour event and was thrilled to be invited by tournament host Miguel Jimenez. Johansen and former Ryder Cupper Andrew Coltart spoke to each other about the way Etchart replaced his market ball on two separate occasions and they both agreed that it was not done according to the rules. However, neither player said anything to Borja on either occasion. Why, for crying out loud, did they not mention something to him after the first time they noticed it?

One would think that the 40-year-old veteran (at the time), Coltart, would have addressed the matter with the young rookie upon noticing the ball marking breach the first time. Information on the Rules is not advice and players are permitted, indeed encouraged, to prevent any breach of the Rules.

Afterwards, a tearful Etchart was adamant that he had not tried to cheat. Through an interpreter he said this: "The two players have seen me doing it wrongly and if that's what they say I take it. But I think I have done nothing wrong. I may have made a mistake, but I think they made a big mistake by not reporting that. They didn't mention anything during the round. I accept this but I feel it was a bad gesture reporting it after I signed my card." Etchart had a right to be ticked off at those two clowns he played with who rained on his parade. This was a tournament in his homeland that he had been looking forward to with great anticipation. He played 18 holes of golf without incident—that he was aware of. Afterwards, Johansen (his marker) signed his card and gave no clue to him that he had done anything wrong. Then, suddenly and out of the blue, an official tells him he's been disqualified. How brutal is that??

Here's a situation where Johansen had no less than three chances to save both Etchart and himself from disqualification but blew them all. The easiest, of course, would have been at the time of the first incident. Before signing the scorecard he could have addressed the issue. That would have kept both of them in the tournament.

Even after the scorecard was signed, both Gary Player and I would have been shrewd enough to save ourselves, had we been in Johansen's predicament. We would have explained that our eyes must have deceived us on those two occasions where we thought we might have seen young Etchart mark his ball improperly. We watched him on every other hole and his marking was exemplary. It makes no sense that a golfer would mark improperly twice, yet do it properly on all the other 16 holes. Our eyes deceived us— that's it (speaking for Coltart as well). How could the official possibly rule against that logic?

Believe it or not, this was Etchart's second disqualified within a six month period for a ridiculous reason. In European Tour prequalifying, the previous fall, the Spaniard was DQ'd under even more bizarre circumstances.

His dad bought him a new push cart to use for pre-qualifying (in lieu of hiring a caddy) and it had a temperature gauge on it. Idiotically, the European Tour doesn't allow them. Apparently, they view temperature gauges in the same light as yardage gauges which is just plain stupid. Whatever happened to the concept of rules officials using a little common sense and compassion before handing out disqualifications? Borja was unaware that the gauge was even on his cart! Worst of all, he was seven shots clear of the qualifying mark with just a round to go. Talk about heartbreaking! The poor kid couldn't catch a break from anyone.

Here's yet another instance where the official could have easily saved this young golfer from disqualification by concluding that no penalty had been incurred due to the fact that the temperature gauge could not, logically, provide him with any advantage over the competition—other than learning what the outside temperature was. But how in the hell is that going to help his game??

Dustin Johnson, 2010 PGA
Not disqualified, but a stupid penalty cost him a title

This had to have been the first and only time in PGA Tour history when a player was penalized for grounding his club in a bunker that he didn't know existed. "I just thought I was on a piece of dirt that the crowd had trampled down," a shell-shocked Johnson said. "I never thought I was in a sand trap. It never once crossed my mind that I was in a bunker." How did Dustin have no clue he was in a bunker?

First of all, the 2010 PGA was played on a windswept Midwestern course called Whistling Straits in Wisconsin.

Wisconsin borders Minnesota—where the 1970 U.S. Open was held at Hazeltine. That year, Dave Hill was in close pursuit of the title for most of the week, before finishing runner-up. Hazeltine was a fairly new course, like Whistling Straits was in 2010, and not up to the quality standards you would expect from a layout that is holding a major.

As it turned out, Hill was the only golfer in the field who had the guts to tell reporters how poor Hazeltine really was: "What Hazeltine lacked was 80 acres of corn and a few cows. They ruined a good farm when they built this course." Even though Hill was fined by the PGA Tour for making those insulting comments, Hazeltine's board of directors took them seriously. A short while later the property was bulldozed over and a total reconstruction of the golf course was undertaken.

Based upon the absurd situation that took place in the 2010 PGA, I think Hill would have been critical of Whistling Straits as well. The PGA Championship must have been held on that god-forsaken property, not once but twice, because

Whistling Straits owner Herb Kohler, the toilet magnet, had a great deal of financial clout.

Back to Dustin Johnson. Granted he must have choked a bit, under the pressure, with his drive on the 72nd hole. He was renowned for being a straight, long driver of the golf ball. But in that instance, he hit a weak flair out to the right that wound up in a particularly scrubby, sandy area in the rough that had been trampled down by thousands of spectators throughout the week.

As Johnson approached his tee shot, there were spectators standing in the sand, in the so-called bunker, no more than a yard from his ball! If this sort of thing had taken place at a true championship course, like Augusta National, people would have been appalled.

Never before in the history of professional golf (except the 2004 PGA at the same Whistling Straits) have spectators been allowed to trample through and stand in a bunker, which is deemed a hazard. Every other respectable course in the world has at least one or two rakes that the player (or his caddie) is required to use for smoothing out the sand, after playing from the bunker. This bunker, like far too many bunkers on this course, had no rakes at all!

Who's responsible for the Whistling Straits PGA Championship bunker blunder? Herb Kohler and Pete Dye, the architect. The maintenance crew must smooth out all the bunkers before the start of play each day. Why would they penalize players, who happen to play later in the day, when certain bunkers are loaded with footprints, without a rake?

Mark Wilson, head of the PGA's rules committee that week, should have had some say in the course set up. He was fully aware that there were numerous bunkers without rakes and, even worse, spectators standing in and trampling through them. Yet, he seemed to believe (insanely) that this was an acceptable for a PGA Championship. Worst, of all, Wilson blamed Johnson for not recognizing that scrubby area was a bunker.

Australian pro golfer Stuart Appleby was angry that the 2010 PGA came to an end the way it did with the penalty on Dustin Johnson. A similar thing happened to Appleby in the 2004 PGA. It was insane that this idiotic stuff had to happen again in 2010. Even I was very upset about it, though I was merely watching it on TV from my stupid couch.

In spite of the 2010 PGA Championship fiasco, that tournament is scheduled to be contested at Whistling Straits *again* in 2015! There are scores of far better sites they could have chosen for the 2015 PGA. Has Herb Kohler been slipping money under the table to the PGA's upper brass or does The PGA of America simply love controversy?

Seriously, I urge every reader to call and write The PGA of America to demand that in 2015 every bunker on Whistling Straits is equipped with a rake and spectators are prohibited from bunkers. **Send your letters to: The PGA of America, 100 Avenue of the Champions, Palm Beach Gardens, FL 33418. Call them at (561) 624-8400.** We can help to make certain the bunker debacle of the 2004 and 2010 PGA Championships will never happen again.

Camilo Villegas, 2011 Tournament of Champions

Happy 29th birthday Camilo. Wait, it's not so happy. We're disqualifying you from the tournament. Villegas posted a 1-under par 72 for his first round on the Kapalua Plantation Course. However, on the par-5 15th hole his second shot landed to the right of the severely elevated green with a tight pin placement. He proceeded to hit a delicate chip shot a little too delicately and it came rolling back to his feet. He learned absolutely nothing from that shot as the same thing happened again on his fourth shot.

The potential penalty arose when he brushed some loose grass away from the area of his divot while the ball was still rolling. Villegas ended up signing for a 7 on the hole, which did not include a two-stroke penalty. Neither his playing partners nor the rules officials noticed that Camilo had violated the rules.

Nevertheless, the head rules official, Slugger White, accepted the opinion of a TV viewer who called in belatedly, contending that Camilo's action violated Rule 23-1, which states: "When a ball is in motion, a loose impediment that might influence the movement of the ball must not be removed."

Yet again, a PGA Tour player was ratted out by a TV viewer. When the hell is the PGA Tour going to stop this insanity of allowing TV viewers to call penalties on players for extremely minor infractions, after they've already signed off on their scorecard? That was something White, who was on the scene, should have caught long before the card was signed. Furthermore, I can't envision how blades of grass would have influenced the movement of the ball. It certainly didn't make his next shot any easier. No penalty should have been assessed.

In the aftermath, White made the moronic comment, "It makes me sick that it wasn't recognized prior to him signing the card." Sadly, the matter could have easily been resolved in Camilo's favor if White had simply given him the benefit of the doubt and concluded that it was unlikely those loose pieces of grass would have influenced the ball's movement. Thus, saving Villegas from disqualification was a no-brainer. In light of Slugger's striking out in this rules officiating blunder, I've renamed him Whiffer. (Let's hope Whiffer never learns the hind-lick maneuver.)

Padraig Harrington, 2011 Abu Dhabi Golf Championship

He was disqualified from the opening event of the season for signing an incorrect scorecard the day after an incredibly minor, almost indiscernible, rules infraction took place. This happened after he turned in an outstanding first round score of 65 that left him one stroke out of the lead.

Insanely, this disqualification was the result of an email that was received by European Tour senior referee Andy McFee from a TV viewer who contended that when Harrington replaced his marked ball on the 7th green, his hand moved the ball a minute fraction of an inch and he failed to replace it.

Upon close examination of TV footage, McFee determined that Harrington's hand did, in fact, move his ball approximately 1/32nd of an inch closer to the hole after replacing his marked ball. However, that is an incredibly minute movement of the golf ball and something a TV viewer could only discern through close up video footage on HD TV.

The big problem we have here is that the movement of the ball was very miniscule and Harrington had no clue that his ball had moved. Undoubtedly, incredibly minor ball movement situations such as that have taken place zillions of times over the years in both amateur and professional golf without the incurrence of penalties. Incidents such as this continue to remind me of how idiotic the rules officiating is in on both the PGA and European Tours. There needs to be, at least, a tiny bit of allowance for human error and recognition that the marking and replacement of a golf ball is not an exact science to a minute fraction of an inch. Furthermore, it's idiotic to contend that Harrington could have obtained any advantage from having moved his ball 1/32nd of an inch closer to the hole.

However, the even bigger argument I have is that belated phone calls and emails from TV viewers should not be allowed to do the officiating that the rules officials failed to perform. In light of this rules enforcement debacle, I'm re-naming the rules official responsible for this mess Andy McFink, as in rat fink.

Simon Dyson, 2013 BMW Shanghi Masters

Dyson of England was greeted with unwelcome news when he arrived at the course for third round play on Saturday morning. He was disqualified from this European Tour event due to a rules violation that he committed on the eighth hole of his second round. This turned out to be a particularly costly infraction due to the importance of this tournament.

At the time, Dyson was in second place with a good chance of victory and a huge payday in this $7 million event. Even worse, it destroyed his golden opportunity of making a big climb up the European Tour money list.

This was the first of four events that made up European Tour's equivalent to the FedEX Cup playoff series. Only the top 60 players made it into $8 million season-ending DP World Tour Championship, which concluded in November and Dyson was ranked 66 at the time. As things turned out, Dyson critically needed a strong showing in that event as he came up short in qualifying for DP World Tour Championship and finished the year in 72nd place on the money list.

The violation occurred on the green on the eighth hole at Lake Malaren, after Dyson marked his ball. He tapped down a repaired ball mark (presumably) that was directly in line with his putt. But that seems like a reasonable thing do, right? Wrong, Simon was found to have breached Rule 16-1a, which states that "a player must not touch his line of putt." This was later confirmed by European Tour Chief Referee John Paramor. Believe it or not, there's a two stroke penalty for that incredibly minor infraction.

Once again a pro golfer was ratted out by TV viewer a day after the golfer's scorecard was signed off on, assuring his disqualification. Will this insanity never end??—both the enforcement of an unfair rule that conflicts with actions that are strongly encouraged by the USGA and allowing TV viewers to call penalties on players.

Let's examine Rule 16-1a a little more closely. Every player knows that golf etiquette requires you to repair ball marks on the green, right? This idiotic rule says that you can't tap down a poorly repaired ball mark that is in your line as that would involve touching your line of the putt. However, it allows a player to further repair that ball mark and then tap it down. The problem is that there are no less than seven exceptions to this rule that are allowable. How much more complicated can a rule get??

Furthermore, what the hell is the purpose of this rule? The only thing I can think of is that the USGA is guarding against the possibility that a player could press down so hard with his putter head that he creates a groove in the putting surface that will assist in guiding the ball to the hole. Isn't that a bit far-fetched?? In all my years of golf, playing thousands of rounds, I've never observed a player doing anything with their putter (other than making a good stroke) that could possibly have helped them hole a putt. Thus, Rule 16-1a is an idiotic rule that needs to be thrown out.

Tiger Woods, shafted in 2013 Masters

On the 15th hole, during Friday's round at a point in which he was tied for the lead, Tiger chose to lay up to about 100 yards short of the green. From there, he hit his wedge shot with such deadly accuracy that it struck the bottom of the flagstick and bounced off the green and into the hazard fronting the green. Had the shot missed the pin, he would likely have had a kick-in birdie. Tiger received a single penalty stroke for that horribly unfair rub of the green, but adding the stroke for replaying the shot, it (effectively) cost him two. Sadly for Tiger, that was just the beginning of his troubles.

Tiger mistakenly took an improper drop two club lengths behind his previous shot, due to mud, believing it was within the rules to do so. However, USGA rule 26-1a states that a player must take their drop "as nearly as possible at the spot from which the original ball was last played". Tiger ended up signing for a one-stroke penalty and a round of 72.

Unfortunately for Tiger, a TV viewer by the name of David Eger who happened to be a former rules official, took it upon himself to rat Tiger out for this minor rules violation so that Woods could be doubly punished for hitting his golf shot too accurately. To make matters even worse, Eger waited until after Tiger signed his scorecard before contacting a Master's rules official which (seemingly) assured Wood's disqualification.

Surprisingly, the Masters committee met with Tiger the following morning and their initial decision was that there was no violation! But they felt the need to discuss the situation further with Woods. Not to be overly hard on those Master's officials, but were they complete morons? Close examination of the video footage clearly showed that Tiger's drop was in violation of the strict USGA rules that govern that situation. Thus, a two-stroke penalty was called for. How could they not understand that and what in the world was there to discuss with Tiger? Ultimately, they came to the historic decision to assess Tiger a two stroke penalty that would be added to his previous day's scorecard—which Tiger accepted, like he was supposed to, right?

NO, that was not the right thing to do, according Greg Norman, who proceeded to rake Tiger over the coals for going along with the rules officials' decision—insisting that it was Tiger's obligation to disregard the official ruling and maintain the sport's etiquette by withdrawing. Then Norman went on to accuse Tiger of having no integrity.

Norman was not alone in that line of thinking as Brandel Chamblee was quick to join in on the Tiger bashing, further condemning him for not disqualifying himself. David Duval chimed in with these moronic comments, "I think he should withdraw. He took a drop to gain an advantage." David, did you really think Tiger was dumb enough to intentionally take an illegal drop, knowing that his every move was being scrutinized?? That would have been an idiotic risk for Tiger to take. A golfer doesn't win 14 majors by being stupid.

Fred Couples was the only renowned Tour player to stick up for Tiger and give the poor guy a break. Couples totally disagreed with the comments of the Tiger bashers, saying the ruling was "one of the best ever." Fred went on to say that the decision had set a "fantastic" precedent to protect players from unwitting mistakes for years to come.

The bottom line is that Couples was right in his assessment of the situation while the other three were wrong. Tour players of today should be grateful that Tiger didn't wimp out and DQ himself, as Norman would have done, making it impossible for that "fantastic" precedent to be set. I go even further in Fred's line of thinking, asserting that neither the assessment of penalties nor disqualification should be allowed after the scorecard has been signed off on. Read on.

Demand drastic change to USGA Rule 33-7!

USGA Rule 33-7 allows golfers to be disqualified for a rules violation committed during the round, that wasn't discovered until after the player's scorecard was signed.

In this chapter, I have described no less than a dozen PGA pros who were disqualified for signing an incorrect scorecard that was believed to be correct at the time. That should never happen unless a player does something dishonest—like what Vijay Singh did in 1985 (see Chapter 15).

In no other sport can a participant be disqualified, after his competition has concluded for the day, due to an innocent mistake on his part during the play. Any rules infraction that takes place during the course of play should be addressed by either the player, one of the playing partners, or a rules official, *before* the scorecard is signed by the player and the scorer.

The only people who should be able to call a penalty on a player are either the player himself, one of his playing partners, or a rules official. If there is a rules violation dispute during the round, it should be settled before the scorecard is signed. If neither the player, nor one of his playing partners, nor an official notices any possible rules violations during the round, it should be too late afterward for a player, whose scorecard is signed, to be penalized.

If a rules violation is observed during the course of play, there is plenty of time for the violation to be addressed before the scorecard is signed. It's unfair for a player to be disqualified, after signing his scorecard, for committing a minor violation of which he was unaware.

And it's not OK for a guy watching a tournament on TV to be able to coax the PGA Tour rules committee into calling a penalty on a player—especially after he has already signed his scorecard. That penalty assessment punishes golfers who have later tee times, or are playing particularly well that given week, because those are the players who are likeliest to get the most TV coverage.

Allowing the home viewer to assess penalties makes it acceptable for rules officials to fail at their jobs. The home viewer can do their job for them. No other sport in the world has TV viewers from home calling penalties on player. Why is golf the only sport where this nonsense is allowed to take place? It's high time the rules and penalty assessments in golf fall in line with every other sport in the world. This is a rules change that should been done with the elimination of stymies.

This simple rule change would hold rules officials responsible for doing their job. Is that too much to ask? Typically, when a player commits a violation and no one else in the group (nor any officials on the scene) notices the infraction, it tends to be a very minor violation that provided the player with no advantage over the rest of the field.

We desperately need to restore the responsibility of penalty enforcement and assessment where they belong—with the player, his playing partners and rules officials.

The rule change I am demanding would have prevented virtually every unfair disqualification that was discussed in this chapter. Players would never again be severely punished with disqualification because the officials were not doing their jobs.

There also are numerous instances in which players, after great contemplation, choose to do the honorable (but stupid) thing and call penalties on themselves, not during the round but days later, assuring their disqualification. With this rule change, it would prohibit these penalties from being assessed. The stymie rule in golf, which was also idiotic and unfair, was eliminated from golf more than 60 years ago. It's high time to change the penalties rule.

How are we going to pressure the USGA to make this important rule change? Through a petition, of course! Please go to the appendix of this book to see this USGA petition, demanding an immediate change to Rule 33-7.

CHAPTER 15

LEGENDARY CONTROVERSIES
AND SCANDALS

Is Gary Player professional golf's most controversial player ever?

In the words of a former tour player who asked to remain anonymous, "I happened to play the tour during Gary's heyday, and there were rumors about his 'bending' the rules all over the place. Many players, not just Watson, knew of his ability to create or improve lies to benefit his performance.

"Though Peter Kessler did a fairly extensive interview on the Golf Channel with a video of the incident at the '74 Open Championship (where Rabbit Dyer found Player's ball seconds before he would have had to declare it lost), nothing definitive was ever produced to disprove his credibility. However, if you watch the video, on the next hole (the 18th and 72nd hole of the championship), Player clearly cheated when his ball came to rest next to the clubhouse. Forced to play a shot left-handed with his putter, he took an initial address over the ball and then looked to the gallery on the roof and asked them to be still so that their shadows didn't distract him. Then, he addressed the ball again, and made a mock

144

practice stroke....an exaggeratedly long stroke, that moved about an inch of soil directly behind the ball in the process. There is no denying this one, as it is as plain as the nose on his face. This improved his lie considerably, and he should have been given a two stroke penalty. To me, that kind of infraction is so obvious to those of us in the profession, it clearly brings the lost ball back into question. I have my doubts, and fear that Rabbit did plant it.

"In the video of the '74 Open championship you can clearly see the R&A members gathered in the balcony above Player as he moved soil on his practice stroke saw it as well. They are clearly heard commenting on his infraction."

These are the words of Jon Gatward. Captain Frinton on Sea golf Club in 1986 and member of the EGU: "In 1974, Rabbit (Gary Player's caddy) dropped a ball for Player at Gary's instruction. A BBC camera man, who saw Rabbit drop the ball, searched and found the real ball player struck. At the dinner after wards, he went to up to Player and said, "Mr. Player I believe this belongs to you."

Here are the words of Gary Player concerning that Open Championship incident: "There are certain things that are possible and certain things that are impossible. First of all, they had the TV cameras on during the whole incident. For anybody to say that Rabbit dropped a ball is dreaming. I would put my life on the fact that he wouldn't do something like that. It's impossible. The grass was so thick."

In his book *To Be The Best*, Player said: "As we walked towards the green I wondered whether we would ever find the ball. The first thing I did was to ask an official to put the watch on me to observe the five-minute rule. I was in full view of the cameras. Imagine winning the Open and then somebody claiming I'd gone seven seconds over my allotted time. It is a unique aspect of golf that anybody anywhere who spots a rules infringement during play can report it and have official action taken. It was a frantic search in which I even got down on my hands and knees looking for the ball. I asked everybody around me to join in the hunt but it still seemed like a hopeless task. There was barely a minute of time left when a marshal found the ball."

Here's a story that was passed down by Florida golfer, Jim Chancey, a veteran tour player who turned pro in the early 1970s. It involves a time in which Jim played with Gary Player in a tournament in England. I believe it took place in 1973—which would make it the year before the Open Championship incident. This was another situation where Gary lost his ball in the rough and the group had been scouring the area for nearly five minutes. Then, suddenly, Rabbit finds the ball when the others aren't watching him. Amazingly, the ball is sitting up nicely in an area of the rough that they had gone back and forth over several times.

Jim seriously considered accusing Gary of drop a ball down as there was no way they could have missed seeing that ball, sitting up like that, in their thorough search efforts. However, Jim was a rookie on tour and Gary was a big star, already with six majors to his credit. Thus, he didn't have the guts to accuse Player who (of course) realized that before he allegedly instructed Rabbit to drop a second ball. Consequently, this was another incident where Gary (officially) did not break the rules as nothing was ever called on him.

There was another very clever incident a decade or so ago in the Senior British Open where Player asked for an official to observe while he, Player, identified his ball in the rough, as the rules allow. Player picked up his ball and identified it before replacing it. The only thing is, his ball was sitting noticeably higher in the rough after this identification. Peter Alliss, was the commentator, along with someone else, and the two got very quiet, the only comment being Aliss's, "Very interesting."

It's been said that one of Gary's favorite tricks when he missed a fairway was to pull out a fairway wood and take a stance behind the ball—tamping the grass down—and then "changing his mind" and deciding to hit an iron. Obviously, this will prevent the twisting irons are subject to when you're hitting down on a ball in the rough—and if you tamp it down enough, you might even be able to give yourself a lie that could enable you to pick the ball clean. That shot just became much easier. But nobody ever called Gary on that sort of thing either.

Finally, Watson calls Player out for cheating and ignites a feud

The only professional golfer to ever seriously call Gary out for cheating was Tom Watson in the 1983 Skins Game in which Nicklaus, Palmer, Player and Watson were paired. On the 244-yard 16th hole, Tom Watson accused Player of illegally uprooting a leaf that obstructed him during a chip shot. From 30 feet away, according to sports writer Dave Anderson, Watson could be heard saying, "I'm accusing you, Gary…you can't do that. I'm tired of this shit. I wasn't watching you, but I saw it."

After the incident, Player managed to get up and down for par, tying Watson on the hole and preventing Watson from winning a $120,000 skin. Palmer was out of the hole and Nicklaus hadn't secured his par yet. On the next hole, Player won the skin money which had then grown to $150,000. It's possible through improving his lie that Player managed the par that may have stolen $120,000 out of Watson's pocket. The gallery saw smoke coming out of Tom's ears.

In a telephone interview the following day, Watson said firmly, "What I saw was a violation. As I saw it, he was moving a leaf of a weed right behind his ball so that he could have a clear path to the ball for the clubface of his club. I know the leaf was rooted because it popped back up to its original position.

"I challenged Gary on it. I asked him if he was ignorant of Rule 17-1 [now 13-2] which states that a player must not improve or allow his lie to be improved." Tom lacked diplomacy, asking a 30-year tour veteran and a leading money winner if he was aware of a basic rule of golf and that infuriated Gary.

On that same hole, Player pulled another clever trick. Instead of using a Titleist he had been playing the entire round, he switched to a harder Pinnacle ball to hit less club to that monster par-3.

Later, Nicklaus questioned rules official Joe Dey whether the "one ball" rule was being used as it is on tour. But there was not much Dey could say—there had been no thought of needing to enforce this rule. I'm sure they expected all four players would be playing by the same rules as the tour. To this day, Player is the only golfer to swap out ball types in Skins Game competition, and get away with it, as always.

To Gary's credit, however, it amazes me that he was able to get up and down from the rough with a ball that checks about as well as an elderly woman who just took up hockey. I played with a Pinnacle one time (back in the early 80s) and was lucky to get a chip within 30 feet of the hole. Frustratingly, that same shot with my Titleist wound balata ball would have wound up stone dead!

Earlier that year, Watson called Player out for tapping down spike marks during a round they played in the Canadian Open. Gary alluded to it in his 1991 book *To Be the Best*, denying doing anything wrong. At the conclusion of the round, Watson reportedly refused, initially, to sign Player's scorecard until he added a two-stroke penalty. However, it was his word against Player's. Watson wound up letting the incident slide and signed the card without the penalty strokes. I could have told Tom there's no way he could call a penalty on Gary Player that would actually stick. Gary's way too smart for that.

Retaliating Watson's accusations, Player took a cheap but rather cunning shot at Tom in *To Be the Best*—saying Watson should forfeit the two majors he won in 1977, the Masters and Open Championship. "I would hate to have won two of the world's major championships," Player writes, "knowing I had used illegally grooved clubs."

It was confirmed that the irons Watson was using were not compliant with the USGA and R&A. But no one, including Watson, had been aware of that. Player went on to call Watson "not half a man." Watson responded by referring to Player as "the little man." Since Gary is only about 5-feet 6 inches, that sounds like a fair description.

Sports columnist Bob Verdi wrote an article in the *Chicago Tribune* titled, "Watson doesn't have to say so: Player is a little man." In his article, Verdi says, "The little man, Player, always is selling himself. He will advertise his accomplishments whenever the spirit moves him, which is all too often. There's no doubt this South African must be mentioned in the same breath with the sport's other legends. If only Player would let his record save his breath. But no such luck.

"Whenever compared with the best ever, Jack Nicklaus, Player routinely prattles on about how his poor body has survived more plane rides than any other athlete's. It's almost as though he thinks miles count as birdies. Or trophies. Your ears can handle this tired refrain. What's new is that Player now strives to sell a book, too. A book that sells the author, of course.

" 'I have to say on a personal level that I have never warmed to Tom (Watson) as a person. I found him too dour,' Player reveals in *To Be the Best*. And that's the gentle stuff. Then Player charges that Watson achieved the 1977 Masters and British Open crowns while swinging weapons that did not conform to specification....Well, now, if that isn't the pot calling the kettle black.

"For all his international success, Player can't shake his notoriety as a golfer long suspected of taking indecent liberties with the rules. He has been involved in several episodes, a few of which he broaches in his autobiography. One brouhaha concerns the original Skins Game of 1983 just outside Phoenix, where Watson accuses Player of removing a live leaf from behind his ball, an infraction. Player swears no to this day.

"Watson imagines that dispute has much to do with St. Gary's literary effort. Watson, indeed, did have his clubs impounded in 1977 after the PGA Tour discovered a manufacturer's error. But Raymond Floyd had to get another set, too, and even Player had to surrender half the irons in his bag. Watson since has won many tournaments while retaining his position as perhaps the most moral, upstanding pro in spikes. Player, meanwhile, comes off as a fellow quite adept at improving his lie in print, too."

Bob Verdi was a staff writer and columnist for the *Chicago Tribune* from 1967 to 1997 before he started freelancing for the newspaper as a contributing columnist. He also served as a senior writer for *Golf Digest* and *Golf World*. In 2004, Verdi received the PGA of America Lifetime Achievement Award in Journalism, which honors members of the media for the steadfast promotion of golf, both locally and nationally, throughout their career.

As players arrived for the 1977 PGA Championship, their clubs were inspected to confirm that their grooves were in compliance with the USGA guidelines. As it turned out, the irons being used by many of the tour players (including Watson) had to be confiscated, due to grooves that were non-compliant. Even Player had several irons that turned out to be illegally grooved. Watson wound up borrowing a 25-year-old set of Tommy Armour Silver Scot irons that Roger Maltbie had sitting in the trunk of his car. Tom managed to shoot a first round of 68 that left him just one stroke out of the lead. Apparently, the grooves didn't make much difference. Perhaps Tom should be allowed to keep his two major victories from 1977 after all. As if Watson, or anyone else in the sporting world, would ever give back trophies—aside from Lance Armstrong.

In Chapter 6 of Dave Hill's book, *Teed Off*, he spoke of a PGA Tour player "high on the list of all-time money winners who advances his ball farther illegally than Jim Brown of the Cleveland Browns." Hill didn't mention any particular player's name, but in that period he could only have been referring to one of the "Big Four"—Nicklaus, Palmer, Player or Casper. We all know it couldn't have been Jack, Arnie or Billy. Who does that leave us with?

There was yet another controversial incident in the Senior British Open involving Player in which he asked for an official to observe while Gary identified his ball in the rough, as the rules allow. Player picked up his ball, "identified" it, then replaced it. Amazingly, his ball was sitting noticeably higher in the rough after this identification. Peter Alliss was the commentator, along with another colleague, and the two got very quiet—the only comment being Alliss saying, "Very interesting." That was Gary in his finest and most clever hour. Improving your lie isn't cheating if the rules official goes along with it, right?

Japanese golf officials gave Ozaki license to cheat?

Greg Norman once accused Jumbo Ozaki of being "creative" with his driver when he saw Ozaki place the club head behind his ball in deep rough, supposedly flattening the grass, before hitting the shot with an iron. A furious Norman was apparently told by the Japan PGA that he can't accuse Jumbo of cheating in Japan and the matter was whitewashed due to Ozaki's celebrity status. Greg, reportedly, refused to sign Jumbo's card at the end of the round—but later relented, finally realizing that Jumbo had the officials in the palm of his hand.

Suspicions of Ozaki cheating run rampant among golf's moral majority—the professional tour caddies. "I've got a friend who says when Jumbo marks his ball it looks like he's playing Chinese checkers," said Jerry Higginbotham, Mark O'Meara's caddie, during a swing through Japan.

Speaking of Ozaki, I was shocked to learn that he was forced to file for bankruptcy in November of 2005 with debts totaling 1.6 billion yen. How is it possible for a former successful pro baseball player and superstar golfer who won 94 (mostly Japanese) tournaments to lose everything plus nearly $13.5 million? If you Include his endorsement income, he had to have lost well over $200 million all total. That makes John Daly's $60 million in gambling losses seem not so bad. It's probably fair to say that, from a financial standpoint, Jumbo Ozaki has to be the biggest disaster in the history of professional golf!

Young Vijay Singh was not immune from cheating

One of the more blatant incidents of cheating in a professional tournament golf belongs to Singh in the 1985 Indonesian Open. He was caught improving his score by a stroke before turning in his card, in order to make the cut. He was subsequently banned from playing on the Asian Tour for three years. In his defense, Vijay was only 22 at the time and no other allegations of cheating have surfaced against him.

Vijay still contends it was a misunderstanding. An American player who was there had this to say, "It was not a misunderstanding. All of us who were around are very upset that Vijay denies this." At least Vijay learned his lesson early in his pro career.

Swedish golfer Johan Tumba improved his scorecard

In 1992, Tumba pulled a stunt similar to Vijay's in a pre-qualifying event in England for PGA Q-School. After shooting a 74, he changed the score on two par-5s, from 5 to 4, and signed for a 72. He was banned for 10 years by the European Tour. He is the son of former Swedish hockey star Sven Tumba, who designed golf courses and lived during the winters in West Palm Beach, before dying in 2011 at age 80.

The ban on Tumba was harsh, considering it was a pre-Q-School qualifying event. I don't condone cheating, but the punishment should fit the crime. A three-year ban, like Vijay's, would have been more appropriate. Nevertheless, Johan was stupid to think none of his playing partners would notice his 74 becoming a 72. The moral of the story: It's never a good idea to assume your playing partners are complete morons.

Ken Venturi and Arnold Palmer

Until his death in 2013, Venturi insisted Palmer knowingly signed an incorrect scorecard, a 3 on a hole when he really scored a 5, on his way to winning the 1958 Masters. On the par-3 12th hole, Arnold flew his tee shot over the green and wound up in a lie that was partially plugged. He asked rules official Arthur Lacey for relief, according to Venturi, but was denied. Arnold went ahead and played out the hole, making double bogey. "I didn't like your ruling," Arnold said, glaring at Lacey. "I'm going to play a provisional ball."

"He was really playing what is called a 'second ball'," Venturi argued. On the second ball Arnold managed to save par. After finishing the 13th hole, Palmer received an unofficial ruling that he won the argument and the 3 would stand.

Two holes later, it was made official. Shaken by the ruling, Venturi bogeyed the 14th, 15th and 16th holes which put him out of the tournament.

Palmer went on to win the Masters by one stroke over Doug Ford and Fred Hawkins. Venturi finished two shots behind Palmer. Sadly (for Venturi) had he kept his emotions in check, accepted the favorable ruling for Arnie, and merely played holes 14 through 16 in even par, he would have won the tournament.

The controversy involved Rule 3-3a which allows a golfer to play a second ball when a dispute arises, but they are to announce their intentions before "taking further action." In his 2004 book, *Getting Up & Down: My 60 Years in Golf*, Venturi writes, " 'You can't do that,' I told him. 'You have to declare a second before you hit your first one. Suppose you had chipped in with the other ball? Would you still be playing a second?' "

Venturi says he confronted Palmer again in the scoring tent. "You're signing an incorrect scorecard," I told him. 'No I'm not,' Arnold replied. 'The ruling was made.' "Venturi claimed that Augusta National co-founders Bobby Jones and Clifford Roberts told him years later that Palmer should not have received the favorable ruling. However, that's difficult to confirm as they've both been dead for over 35 years.

I would never accuse Arnold Palmer of cheating, considering everything Arnie has meant to the game and how he's renowned for being a man of great

integrity—especially not over one incident that took place more than 50 years ago. But a photo taken at the time of the incident (on the previous page) is eerie. And *Golf Week,* in September of 2004, takes notice of the long-ago incident with an online article headlined "Venturi writes that Palmer cheated."According to an Aug. 9, 2008, *Sports Illustrated* article headlined "1958 Masters: Arnie's Army is born," this photo is Ken Venturi and Arnold Palmer speaking with rules officials at the 12th hole during the 1958 Masters. It looks an awful lot like Bobby Jones and Clifford Roberts in the golf cart, not Arthur Lacey by himself, who Venturi stated was the rules official making the 12th-hole ruling. Arnold received a ruling on that hole, supposedly by Mr. Lacey, that he was not entitled to a drop. Unhappy with the ruling and the double bogey that resulted, Arnold played a second ball that resulted in a par. Three holes later, a rules official sided with Arnold and allowed the free drop and resulting par to stand.

If Arnold had received the initial ruling from Jones and Roberts, at the 12th hole, they would have known the correct ruling and Arnold wouldn't have questioned it. It contradicts Venturi's story that Jones and Roberts didn't learn about it until years later.

The photo appears to be of an incident that never actually happened—straight out of the "Twilight Zone." I keep looking for Rod Serling standing somewhere in the background—as if I'm reading one of those *Highlights* magazines for children that you find in dental offices, with hidden beings lurking in the oddest places.

Even more mysterious is the *Sports Illustrated* article that says Bobby Jones, himself, gave Arnold the official ruling on the 15th hole. Then what are Bobby Jones and Clifford Roberts doing talking to Palmer and Venturi on the 12th hole, where the incident allegedly took place?

Fred Couples on the 12th hole Augusta National again, in the final round of the 1992 Masters doing a no-no.

Fred Couples, 1992 Masters

Using a strict interpretation of the rules of golf, Couples was (arguably) guilty of multiple rules-breaking blunders in the 1992 Masters on the 12th hole that no one called him on! He scoops up another ball out of the water and chips it back in—which could be construed as playing the wrong ball, practicing during the round and testing a hazard. These infractions are all two-stroke penalties and he knew it instantly, watching his reaction. He should be embarrassed every time he sees it. The question is, how many penalty strokes should Fred have been assessed? (It's a trick question.)

Actually, the number of penalty strokes is irrelevant because Couples signed for a score that didn't include any penalties for his rule-breaking on the 12th hole. He should have been disqualified for signing an incorrect scorecard, instead of winning the Masters with a 275, and Ray Floyd should have been declared the winner. That would have left Fred without a major to his credit and little chance of entering the Hall of Fame, unless he pretended to be Isao Aoki. It also would have cost him the $270,000 winner's check.

If Stadler or Azinger had committed the same violations, phones at Masters' headquarters would have been ringing off the hook. But the golf world was madly in love with Freddy and he could do no wrong. It's hard not to love a guy so nonchalant about leading the Masters, with less than nine holes to play, like it was a walk in the park on a rather boring day.

Where was Mike Shea when Ray Floyd needed him to call a penalty on Couples? Out to lunch, I presume. Please don't tell me he was performing his hind-lick maneuver again!!

Did Kenny Perry pretend he didn't improve his lie?

In the 2009 Phoenix Open Perry was on the first hole of a playoff, preparing to hit a chip shot from a bad lie in the rough. His ball is barely visible on footage shot by a cameraman standing behind him. David Feherty, the on-course TV commentator says, "Kenny has got a lie—it's a down-grain lie but there is a big clump of down-grain grass behind it. I'm not sure he can get the sand wedge on the ball here without playing some kind of muffled shot."

Perry appears to tap his sand wedge behind the ball three times in quick succession and suddenly his ball comes into view. After Perry steps back to study his shot again, two-thirds of the ball is now clearly visible. Brandel Chamblee, former Tour player and analyst with the Golf Channel said, "When I first heard stories about the video I thought, 'I hope Kenny is not being maligned.' And then when I saw it, I was shocked...But I was also shocked that no one who was watching at home called in, or that no one who was doing the television coverage mentioned anything about it on air."

John Paramor, chief referee of the European Tour, has watched this video more than a hundred times, often in the company of other golf pros. "The first thing they say when they see it is: 'The guy has done something bad,' " said Paramor. Later that week, Mark Russell, a senior PGA rules official, whitewashed the incident issuing a short statement: "When a question was raised this week, several members of the tournament committee reviewed the videotape of Kenny Perry and no evidence of any rules violation was found. As the competition is closed, we will have no further comment on the matter."

A two-minute video of the incident was uploaded to the internet for the whole world to see. It was obvious that the ball moved after Perry addressed it. The lie was certainly much improved when he went back to play the shot. That along with Feherty's comments on how bad the lie was, initially, convinces me that Perry moved the ball after addressing it.

Scottish writer John Huggan wrote, regarding Perry: "Collectively, the PGA Tour brass are past masters at making bad news go away, even when the evidence to the contrary is seemingly incontrovertible." It was clear that after Perry jabbed his wedge behind his ball three times, the ball popped up to a much improved lie. Perry had to notice the dramatic lie improvement and it meant he could play a much easier, more straightforward chip shot, rather than an explosion shot. But with Perry's aw-shucks-I-didn't-notice-anything demeanor, people believed him.

Perry improved his lie, then proceeded to play from that improved lie, unto the green. When it was time for Perry to putt, he had had plenty of time to realize the rule violation he made and admit it. That would have put Perry out of the hole and in a second-place finish. The difference between first and second place was $432,000. Bobby Jones probably would have said Perry robbed a bank and got away with a major heist.

In fairness to Kenny, it was (arguably) smart of him to pretend not to notice his improved lie as he had nothing to lose and everything to gain. Furthermore, anyone who says cheaters never win is living in a fantasy world. I'm not saying, without a doubt, that Kenny cheated. You can decide that for yourself.

What's most shocking is millions of people had to have witnessed this improvement in Kenny's lie, but no one bothered to call a penalty. I would have at least expected Mike Shea to contact Perry, a day or two later, to inform him of the penalty—that's the way he normally operates. However, he may still be pondering that incident, contemplating whether to not to call a penalty on Perry.

Norman calls out McCumber for cheating

In the first round of the 1995 Northeast Conference World Series of Golf, at Firestone Country Club, Greg Norman and Mark McCumber were paired. On the par-3 seventh hole, Norman accused McCumber of cheating by pulling out a small clump of grass that was in his line and tamping it down with his finger. McCumber denied the charge, claiming it was just a bug he pulled out of the grass. Later, rules officials sided with McCumber as they had no way to prove he was not telling the truth. Norman was furious and refused to sign McCumber's scorecard.

Reportedly, after the incident Faldo met Norman at some formal function and started brushing his shoulder, claiming there was a spike mark on his jacket. I think most players sided with Norman and McCumber's reputation took a blow. I'm guessing it was mostly forgotten—until now. Sorry Mark.

Pro golf's worst cheater?

My nomination for this dubious award goes to David Robertson. He was guilty of the all-time craziest cheating in professional golf or even any golf. Robertson was a former Scottish boys champion and up-and-coming young golfer, back in the 1980s. David, then 28, was playing in the final qualifying for the 1985 Open in Deal, Kent. After 14 holes, his playing partners flagged down a rules official and after a lengthy discussion the official disqualified Robertson for repeatedly failing to replace his ball anywhere near the correct position on the green.

It was estimated that, at times, he moved his ball up to 20 feet or more. He did this by literally running up to the green ahead of his playing partners, appearing to mark his ball, but merely picking it up, carrying his marker on his putter around the green and dropping it much closer to the hole.

He was fined £7,000 and banned for 20 years from playing as a pro by the PGA European Tour. However, the fine was never collected. Caddie Paul Connolly, 20, who handed Robertson's golf bag to a replacement after nine holes, said: "I walked off because I couldn't stand what I was seeing."

"It is a sad day for golf," said Ken Schofield, executive director of the European Tour.

Let me get this straight, Schofield. Wild cheating by a no-name Scottish golfer, playing in a qualifying round for some insignificant Open in Deal, Kent, was important enough to call it a sad day for golf?

Still, banning a guy from playing on The European Tour for 20 years was a ridiculous punishment for Robertson's golf crime, as was fining him £7,000 for cheating in a round of qualifying for an unimportant tournament.

Robertson reportedly was seen (not in this photo) wearing a Titleist cap. Subsequently, they offered him a contract—Titleist is paying him to not wear anything with the name Titleist on it. (My condolences to Callaway.) Sadly, because he remains in such ill repute in the Scottish golfing circles, he's forced to wear a disguise every time he plays golf. But, David, couldn't you come up with something a little less hideous?

David Robertson

I don't care what they say about you, David, I'm sticking up for you. I think a 20-year ban on a young and dumb 28-year-old was way too much. In the same year Vijay got off with a three-year ban. Five years for Robertson would have been appropriate.

Since 29 years have passed (as of this writing), it's a bit late to file an appeal. But he may be able to land a role on the TV series the "Walking Dead." Plus, the Robertson cheating incident provided an excellent story for this chapter.

Bob Toskey admits to cheating?

In 1986, the *Los Angeles Times* ran the headline, "Toskey admits to cheating, quits tour."

However, Toskey, then 59, didn't quite admit to that. What he said was, eloquently, "It is possible that, inadvertently, I did not observe proper ball marking procedures and thereby may have been violating the rules of the game." But how could a veteran golf pro and member of the World Teachers Hall of Fame *inadvertently* fail to observe proper marking procedures?

Toskey quit the Senior Tour promptly after. I'm sure he was happy to go back to teaching, pretending he never played on the Tour. Bob is actually a great guy and, sadly, at 87 as of this writing, he's unlikely to be with us many more years. It's a shame that he wasn't as clever as you-know-who.

Toskey student Jane Blalock accused of cheating

Fourteen years earlier than Toskey's incident, Blalock was accused of cheating by failing, like her teacher, to employ proper ball marking. How ironic is that?? Regardless, moving the ball an inch closer to the hole couldn't possibly make much of a difference and is certainly not worth the risk of ruining one's reputation and career.

Toskey and cheating resurface

In March of 2012, Toskey said he thought the USGA should outlaw the use of long putters. "The Scottish have a word for that—cheating," Toskey said on "Golf Exchange," a South Florida-based radio show. He would know a thing or two about cheating on the putting green. But using a long putter is still not cheating, Bob.

Scotsman Elliot Saltman was also involved in ball marking scandal

Elliot Saltman was accused of incorrectly marking his ball on the putting green at least five occasions in the first round of the September 2012 Russian Challenge Cup in Moscow. After the round, his two playing partners, Stuart Davies and Marcus Higley, raised concerns first with Saltman and then with the tournament referee, Gary Butler, insisting that they wouldn't sign the Scot's scorecard.

Saltman was banned from golf on the European Tour for three months. He got off easy. He has a reputation of taking liberties with the rules on numerous occasions, over many years, to the point where a number of players have refused to sign his card and won't play with him.

My question is this: When did Saltman become a student of Bob Toskey?

Shocking case of cheating by Hall of Fame instructor

As Toskey demonstrated, PGA teachers are not immune to cheating scandals. Northern Chapter PGA teacher David Bartoe was disqualified from the Amelia Invitational in September of 2009, in Jacksonville, Florida, after two competitors saw him kick his ball from behind a tree on the par-4 sixth hole of the Golf Club of Amelia Island. Bartoe, a contract instructor at the World Golf Hall of Fame PGA Tour Academy no less, violated Rule 18-2, prohibiting players from making contact with a ball at rest with anything except a club.

Golfplex Director of Instruction Mark Spencer, one of the witnesses, called it "shocking." Bartoe's now with Advantage Golf School in Orlando. I'm guessing the World Golf Hall of Fame Academy decided they wanted nothing more to do with Mr. Bartoe. His business phone number is toll-free (877) 239-6609—it's a free call if you feel like giving him a hard time about his ball-kicking incident.

Mark O'Meara and Jarmo Sandelin

In the 1997 Trophie Lancome in Paris, Sandelin accused O'Meara of cheating by marking his ball a half-inch ahead of his mark on the 15th hole. Sandelin called him "Mark It Nearer." O'Meara won, and later admitted his mistake after reviewing the video. He kept the trophy and money, though. It's widely believed this rule violation was an innocent mistake by O'Meara.

Say sayonara to your golf career, Ai Takinami

In 2006, this 26-year old golf pro got a 10-year ban from both playing on the Japanese LPGA and teaching golf for profit, when she admitted to improving her scores on two holes, after her marker had signed her scorecard during the first round of the second JLPGA qualifying tournament. This was akin to a death sentence for her career.

**Ai Takinami's
JLPGA Tour photo**

Vijay got three years for doing much the same thing. Does one brief cheating incident, in a qualifying event, justify ending a golf career? The stunt Ai pulled was stupid—thinking her playing partners weren't going to notice her improved scorecard. But I'm sticking up for her— a 10-year ban was cruel and brutal punishment for an isolated cheating incident. A three-year ban would have been sufficient and it wouldn't have destroyed the golf career of a young woman.

And a ban from teaching? Were they worried she was going to teach other golfers how to cheat and destroy their careers? Were they intent on crippling this young woman's chances of earning a livelihood? If a famous male Japanese golfer and cheater, like Jumbo, had been caught committing that same offense, Japanese rules officials likely would have allowed him to add the two strokes back on his card and pretend that he never tried to cheat.

I'm tempted to send my good buddy, Steven Seagal, to Japan to put a "hurtin" on those cold-hearted rules officials so that they can learn the meaning of the word *ruthless*. Afterward, Steven and I will pretend we're R&A Chief, Peter Dawson. We'll accept blame (or take credit) for the beatings but refuse to take responsibility for the injuries that were inflicted.

Australian cheater Luke Kershaw

In 2007, Queensland's Kershaw cheated four times more blatantly than Vijay 1985! He improved his score by four stokes (to a 64) after signing his card for a 68 and was initially named the winner of the Port Sorell Pro-Am. But the Australasian PGA was informed the following day by his playing partners what he did. Kershaw was disqualified and suspended for two years from all professional golf events in Australasia. Kershaw also was required to write a letter of apology to the Port Sorell Golf Club and his playing partners. He shot an excellent round of golf that he should have been proud of.

This young Australian idiot gets only a two-year ban from playing tournament golf for (insanely) taking four strokes off his score card, making him the tournament champion (momentarily). In contrast, a year earlier the young Japanese woman, who improved the score on her card by just two strokes, in a qualifying event just to make the cut, receives a 10-year ban from both playing tournament golf as well as teaching golf. How unfair is that monstrous discrepancy in penalty enforcement?? That does it! I'm sending Seagal on the next available flight to Nippon!

Young Kim whiffs a one-inch putt

It seems that certain Korean women on the LPGA Tour have a thing for cheating. In the 2007 Ginn Open, Kim, a top young Korean golfer on the LPGA Tour, left a putt on the lip of the hole and, in frustration, whiffed on her tap-in attempt, totally missing the ball. She tried to pretend it didn't happen, but one of her playing partners wasn't feeling charitable and called her on the whiff. Young continued denying the missed tap-in attempt, even after they reached the scoring tent—claiming it was merely a practice stroke. Sure, on a 1-inch putt? Her marker decided to accept that crazy explanation and her scorecard got signed, attested and turned in, without the whiff counted.

After a change of heart, Young recanted. However, since the scorecard had already been turned in, it was too late. Thus she was disqualified for signing an incorrect scorecard. At least she didn't get banned for 10 years.

Shi Hyun Ahn & Ilmi Chung: Korean cheating collusion

Possibly the only cheating collusion in professional golf involved two Korean competitors cheating together on the same hole on the LPGA Tour. It was on the 18th hole in the 2010 Canadian Women's Open. Here's how LPGA caddie Larry Smich describes what happened: "Both balls were in the fairway. Ahn missed the green and Ilmi hit hers on. Ahn chipped it close and tapped in for par. This is where it all begins. Ahn noticed that this was not her ball and conversed in Korean with Ilmi. In the meantime, at least one caddie in the group noticed it also but did not say anything."

They finished the hole, went to the scoring tent, checked the scores and signed their cards. According to Smich, "Somewhere, either before or after going to the tent, Ahn told her caddie (a Nationwide looper and only working for her this week), 'You did not see anything.' Ahn and Chung were later disqualified for signing the wrong scorecard." Smich called for the women in the so-called conspiracy to be handled in the "harshest manner possible." He went so far as to suggest lifetime banishment. However, no further action was taken against either of them.

Don't tell me Monty cheated too!

So what happened in Jakarta, at the 2005 Indonesian Open, that causes at least one person to refer to Colin Montgomerie as a cheater? Scottish writer John Huggan tells the story: "It's the second round. Monty needs a very high finish—at minimum, Top 3—to move into the Top 50 world rankings and get into the field at The Players Championship. He's not having a good round.

"And on the 14th hole, Monty put his approach shot into a greenside bunker. The ball was in a bad spot, near the edge of a deep bunker, and Montgomerie struggled to take a stance. He wanted to have both feet outside the bunker, but he couldn't find a stance that worked without having one foot in, and one foot out. Meanwhile, the weather had been worsening, black clouds had been rolling in and before Montgomerie could play the bunker shot the horn sounded, warning golfers and fans of potentially dangerous weather, and stopping play. Monty did not mark his ball in the bunker, he simply left the ball where it lay. And he skedaddled off the course.

"Play didn't resume until the following day, and when Monty returned to that bunker by the 14th green, his golf ball was gone. Stolen. Vanished. We're OK up to this point. No violation of any rule has occurred. What Monty did next is where the controversy arises. Monty consulted with his playing partners and then replaced a golf ball where he estimated his original ball had been. Then he played the shot. So what's the problem? The problem is that Sandy Lyle had seen the position of the original ball and believed that Montgomerie replaced the second ball in a more advantageous position. Lyle contacted the European Tour and told them Monty had replaced the ball in the wrong spot.

"Sandy had been watching the day before on TV while Monty struggled to take his stance. The day before, Lyle noted, Monty couldn't find a stance in which both feet were outside the bunker. But after replacing the stolen ball, on TV, he had no trouble taking a stance outside the bunker, and played an easy chip shot. Clearly, Monty had placed the ball in the wrong spot—a location that was to his advantage, that improved his lie, and that made his stance easy and the shot easier.

"Did he do so intentionally? That's where the cheating accusation comes in. Lyle felt Monty had to know what he was doing in moving the ball an estimated foot or so away from its original spot. He had to have known because it was 1 foot or so, rather than a matter of a few inches; and surely it would have clicked to him that his stance was suddenly very easy. Monty cheated. That's what fellow Scot Sandy Lyle believed and still believes today."

That is the brutally honest account from fellow Scot John Huggan. Monty plays in a tournament 10,000 miles from home and the player who calls him out on a minor technicality is fellow countryman Sandy Lyle? Considering how it wasn't a serious violation one would think a savvy, old Scottish sports writer like Huggan would stick up for Monty.

Monty shrewdly managed to defuse the situation by declaring that his winnings from this event, €34,700, would be donated to a charitable cause. But he could have come up with a more believable charity than the European Tsunami Relief Fund—I'm pretty sure Europeans aren't victimized by tsunamis a hell of a lot. My guess is the true beneficiary of his charity was the Colin Montgomerie Relief Fund.

A caddie in the bush

In June of 2012, Spaniard Jose Manual Lara was disqualified due to stupidity and a bumbling attempt at cheating on behalf of his caddie, Vincent. It's the job of every caddie to make sure there isn't an extra club in the bag before the start of every tournament round. But for some reason, Vincent overlooked this detail. It wasn't until the second hole that the caddie noticed the extra club. At this point, Vincent should have informed Lara about his screw up. Lara could have announced the mistake, added four strokes to his score and continued on with his play. But instead of taking the easy way out, Lara's caddie went bananas, disappearing into a bush—with the bag—to get rid of the 15th club.

Lara assumed that Vincent was going into the bushes to pee. The bigger problem for Vincent was that playing partners Damien McGrane and Peter Hedblom were watching and asked what the hell he was doing. He was stuttering before he finally admitted to the blunder.

"It was clear the club was out of the bag and in the bush at the time. He admitted it straight away and regretted his action," commented European Tour Chief Referee John Paramor. Lara and his caddie ended up disqualified for what Paramor called a "serious incident and warranted disqualification. It was clearly the caddie doing what he felt at the time was the right thing, but was clearly the wrong thing," he told *Sky Sports*. "He's kind of been asked not to come back and that's how the matter has been resolved."

I think it's fair to say that there's *no way Jose* will let Vincent tote his bag again.

Long putters are for "cheaters"

Peter Senior was furious with failed Aussie tour player Mark Allen, who called Senior a "cheat" for using the broomstick putter in December of 2012, following the anchoring ban adoption by golf's ruling bodies. It's perfectly legal to use that putting method until at least January of 2016, if not forever (see Chapter 16).

Falsely branded a cheater, Peter Senior wins Australian Open

Senior won the Open in December of 2012, at 53, with his teenage son, Mitchell, caddying for him. While studying the names on the trophy, Senior remarked, "I don't see Allen's name anywhere on the trophy." You won't see Mark Allen's name on any professional golf trophy because he never won anything.

Conclusion of the Gary Player chronicles

Gary Player is an idol of mine in many ways. The only thing he could do to make me like him more would be to publicly apologize to my friend Tom Watson, for calling him "not half a man" and for other disparaging comments about Tom in his book, *To Be the Best*. Perhaps Gary and Tom could actually become friends again. If that happens, the golf world would have me to thank.

I would love to see Gary and Tom play a friendly round of golf together without worrying about the pesky rules of the game. That way it would be hard for Tom accuse Gary of cheating and they could simply enjoy a delightful round. That is, if Tom could withstand Gary boasting about how he is 79 going on 40.

Gary comes up again in cheating stories

It happened again in 2007! This time it was Gary accusing golfers of using performance- enhancing drugs. Monty didn't take kindly to it and couldn't believe this kind of drug would benefit a pro golfer anyway. Colin suggested Player was out of his mind when he sparked the controversy—without evidence—on the eve of the British Open, claiming top touring pros were pulling a Lance Armstrong.

Even Player's fellow countryman Retief Goosen was dismayed at Gary, commenting that Player must have been referring to golfers in Player's heyday of the '60s and '70s—when Arnold Schwarzenegger admitted to using PIDs. I'll give Gary a break and say that maybe he was having a senior day.

Regardless of whether Gary may have improved his lie from time to time, winning 166 professional tournaments was an incredible accomplishment—especially for a man of short stature. I don't think it's even possible to win that many pro golf events. Somehow Gary did it anyway. I've heard he may have won as many as 167. Apparently, when you win that many tournaments, it's hard to keep track.

I also have tremendous admiration for Gary's fitness; he was a role model for me. He's truly a hero of mine and I would love to meet him and shake his hand. And it would be great if Gary would tell me, privately, who the pro golfers were using those drugs. Gary, you can rest assured I would keep that information confidential.

World Golf Hall of Fame debacles

With no major titles and or PGA Tour wins to his credit, Colin Montgomerie was inducted into the World Golf Hall of Fame in 2013 despite having no PGA Tour wins nor majors to his credit. Maybe the Scottish Hall of Fame. But the World Hall? Furthermore, how could they have the gall to induct Monty ahead of Mark O'Meara, whose seven years older, has two majors to his credit and 16 PGA Tour wins?

Ray Floyd was also upset about it, saying he feels the Hall of Fame is losing its integrity and that all inductees should have a couple of majors to their credit. Nick Faldo believes the special nature of the Hall is being lost on recent inductees with lesser careers than inductees of the past.

Even worse than Monty's induction was that of Japanese golfer Jumbo Ozaki in 2011. Ozaki never won a single golf tournament in either the U.S. or Europe. At least Monty came close to winning majors on three occasions before he choked. Ozaki rarely played in the majors and never finished in a major's top five. Most of his tournaments wins were on the Japanese tour. Additionally, Greg Norman claims Ozaki's has been a prolific cheater in tournament play.

Idiotic controversies in professional golf

The most insanely stupid comments made in the history of pro golf by a male golfer were those made by Fuzzy Zoeller during the 1997 Masters. This, of course, was the year that 21 year old Tiger Woods blew away the field in winning by 12 strokes.

Speaking to reporters at the Masters (past champion) Fuzzy commented, "That little boy is driving well and he's putting well. He's doing everything it takes to win. So, you know what you guys do when he gets in here? You pat him on the back and say congratulations and enjoy it and tell him not serve fried chicken next year. Got it?" Then Zoeller smiled, snapped his fingers, and walked away while adding, "or collard greens or whatever the hell they serve."

Fuzzy's joke wasn't the least bit humorous, it sounded prejudicial and he mislabeled Tiger who happens to be one-third Asian and one-third caucasian. I'm pretty sure Asians are not renowned for eating fried chicken.

As a result of those racist sounding comments, Fuzzy lost his million dollar per year endorsement contract with Kmart—which was a good thing. How insane was it that a two-time major winner was recommending that people purchase their golf clubs from a cheap discount store selling poor quality merchandise through store clerks who know nothing about either golf or golf clubs?

The following day, Fuzzy apologized profusely for making a bad joke. After which, Brad Faxon (the PGA Tour player representative) scrambled to obtain an acceptance from Tiger (who went on vacation) of Fuzzy's apology. That was a mistake. Reason being: Anything that draws more attention to the PGA Tour is guaranteed to increase TV ratings of golf telecasts. Thus, if they had been smart, the Tour would have let this controversy drag on as long as possible and still (today) the TV announcers should be pondering (out loud) whether or not Tiger will ever accept Fuzzy's apology.

In sympathy with Jan Stevenson, it annoys me to see little Asian robots, who never miss a shot, dominating the LPGA Tour. Jan went so far as to say that the Asians are killing the LPGA Tour. She, apparently, would like to see Asian woman banned from playing golf in the U.S. altogether. However, that seems a tad bit harsh to me.

Being open-minded, I think it would be fair to simply limit the number of Asian women to a quota of two or three per LPGA event. Once we determine that precise number we can formulate a petition demanding that LPGA Commissioner Whan put our Asian women quota in place for the start of the upcoming year. Nothing could be any fairer than that, right? But please don't tell me that Commissioner Whan is Asian!!!

The stupidest golf related comment I ever heard in my life (aside from Fuzzy's) was when Stephenson, back in 2003, said she was inspired by Annika's play at the Colonial. Sure, it makes a lot of sense to be inspired by seeing the top LPGA Tour player miss the 36-hole cut (by four strokes) in a PGA Tour event on one of the shorter, tighter courses on the Men's Tour—ideally suited to Annika's game. What should have been particularly embarrassing to the LPGA's #1 golfer is that (unheralded) guys who missed the cut by a single stroke were admitting that their game stunk. But, at least, Annika's ridiculous charade only lasted two days.

Anyway, Annika's dismal failure inspired (51 year old) Jan to play in a Champions Tour event at Turtle Bay in the fall of that same year (in which there was no cut) where she turned in scores of 80, 84, 78, for a +26 total that put her solidly in last place and 34 strokes behind the winner, Hale Irwin—who else? I'm pretty sure that the 8 or 9 handicap golf Jan played to (in those three rounds) was not up to professional standards and that half of the caddies who were toting bags that week probably could have beaten her—playing with gutta percha balls! In fact, Jan's play sucked so bad it made Annika's missing the cut by four strokes look like a sterling performance. Let's face it, these two woman (especially Jan) had no business, whatsoever, playing on the men's tours—unless that business involved making Vijay Singh look like a genius for condemning such idiocy.

I feel its best, however, for Jan to be remembered for her 16 LPGA Tour wins and three major championship victories—not for her idiotic comments nor her zero for 4 playoff record. Actually, I'm a bit surprised she has failed to make it into the World Golf Hall of Fame. Apparently the requirements for women are a bit stiffer than they are for men. She was also a mighty fine looking woman back in the '70s and '80s. In fact, (as of this writing) I still find Jan to be quite attractive. Admittedly, though, my standards of beauty have taken a nosedive in recent years.

CHAPTER 16

CIRCUMVENTING USGA'S ANCHORED PUTTING BAN FOR 2016

Attention USGA: Based on the language of Rule 14-1b, unless a golfer is playing shirtless, he can continue anchoring the putter indirectly against his stomach, chest or sternum, any way he damn well pleases, and comply with this ridiculous rule.

A lot of commotion has been raised about Rule 14-1b, but there's nothing for anybody to worry about. My broomstick is the only putter that I own. Yet, I'm glad this proposed rule change is becoming effective in 2016—I'll have fun circumventing it every time I play golf.

Let's examine Rule 14-1b.

USGA Rule 14-1b Anchoring the Club

In making a stroke, the player must not anchor the club, either "directly" or by use of an "anchor point."

Note 1: The club is anchored "directly" when the player intentionally holds the club or a gripping hand in contact with any part of his body, except that the player may hold the club or a gripping hand against a hand or forearm.

Note 2: An "anchor point" exists when the player intentionally holds a forearm in contact with any part of his body to establish a gripping hand as a stable point around which the other hand may swing the club.

Although these four images look very similar, I'm holding the top hand slightly differently in each one. In this first photo I'm using the broomstick putter and pressing my top hand against my shirt which is against my body. Since my hand is not "directly" touching my body, this method is compliant with the precise wording of rule 14-1b.

Here I'm pressing my top hand against my shirt

Until the USGA rewrites this new rule, all long putter users can continue anchoring their putter as usual—unless they're weird like Sam Torrance and anchor to their chin. Even if the USGA rewrites this new rule (which could be done no sooner than the year 2020) to say that you cannot press your hand against your clothing, I've devised three ways of circumvent a wording change such as that, allowing you to continue using your broomstick as successfully as ever, forever.

Alternative anchoring method No. 1

As in this photo, keep your elbow of the arm holding the top of the putter in a locked position, and your hand slightly held away from the body. With the elbow locked in place, you're able to get the feel of being anchored, while conforming to the rule. Stroking through with the right hand should be your only concern.

Alternative anchoring method No. 2

Here I'm anchoring with my wrist pressed against my sternum, while my hand and forearm are away from my body, within Rule 14-1b parameters. Although it's a bit awkward at first, I've found I can anchor just as securely with the wrist as I can with my hand. Furthermore, with the top hand away from my sternum, it's at a more perpendicular angle to the ground—which is a plus.

Alternative anchoring method No. 3

This one is the most creative of the three. It involves grabbing your shirt in the sternum area with the hand that is holding the top of the putter grip. This will give you the feel of being anchored, while conforming to Rule 14-1b. This method looks a little funny but I think it may be the best one of all for putting with the broomstick—if you don't mind wrinkling your shirt a bit.

If you pull tightly on your shirt, it's virtually impossible for your left hand to waver while making your stroke and it causes the putter to be more vertical to the ground—for a perfect (or close to it) pendulum stroke. You should never have any flinching or yips with this method of putting.

The nice thing about this method is it locks the top hand in place. It works especially well if you're wearing a jacket or wind shirt—the stiffer the clothing, the better to lock your top hand. Then you only need to concern yourself with the bottom hand.

Enforcing 14-1b may be impossible

Besides the wording about clothing vs. the body, when using the broomstick putter it should be legal to hold your top hand lightly against your shirt or slightly away from it as long as the club is not anchored to your body. However, when doing so, it is virtually impossible for your playing partners to be able to determine whether you are anchoring the club and breaking the rule. Should my playing partners have to stand next to me to scrutinize whether my top hand is touching my body? That would be ridiculous.

Peter Senior, like a number of other players, believes the biggest concern, once anchoring of the putters is outlawed, is policing the new policy. "On a day like today when it is very windy, and if you have the putter like this [holding it close to his body] and your shirt is blowing against your hands, who is to know if you are not anchoring the club? You could have any number of your competitors complaining 'Oh, I saw him anchor the club against his body.'" How ridiculous is a rule that is as utterly confusing as that?

The belly putter

On the next page is Leo Diegel using the first belly putter method in 1924. It's idiotic to ban a putting method that has been legal for at least 90 years. The first thing I notice about Diegal is that my back hurts just from looking at the picture. For crying out loud Leo, couldn't you find someone to build you a longer putter? Nicklaus similarly crouched over in his non-anchored putting pose. It's no surprise that he required seven injections in his back for pain by age 19, and suffered from back pain throughout his career.

Another way to get around the anchored putting ban with the belly putter is to learn Fred Couples' technique which dramatically transformed his putting. Fred holds the butt end of the putter against his shirt, which touches his stomach.

Here's Leo Diegel using the first belly putter method in 1924

However, the handle of the club moves back and forth freely during the stroke in a non-anchored fashion. It can't be considered anchoring if the putter is not anchored in any way. Nevertheless, I strongly prefer the broomstick.

Broomstick vs. belly

Any golfer using the belly putter would be better off switching to the broomstick. The broomstick has one significant advantage—it allows you to stand fairly upright, eliminating back strain. Even though Adam Scott's putting has improved with the broomstick, he appears to bend over more than necessary using it. If Adam were to switch to a slightly longer putter and stand closer to the ball, and more erect like I do, this would improve his alignment and his putting. I'd be happy to give Adam a lesson on how the Broomstick Putting Master does it.

Because I use a 50-inch putter and stand fairly close to the ball, I'm able to keep my spine relatively erect. This allows me to practice for hours on end without back strain. But I don't need to. In fact, I spend very little time practicing my putting these days. My alignment and stroke are virtually automatic. The only things I'm concerned with are the speed of the putt and the amount of break, if any.

My putting is so consistently strong I couldn't imagine using anything other than a broomstick putter for the rest of my life—not to mention its advantage when I need to take a club-length drop. It's the Holy Grail of putting.

My final comment, in reference to Rule 14-1b, is that it's as crazy as LADY GAGA's fashion statements. Thus, I think it would be appropriate for golf's governing body in the U.S. to change its name slightly to USGAGA.

And now for a shameless pitch from our sponsor

I can take a golfer who is plagued with the dreaded yips, or is, simply, a bad putter, and transform his or her putting in one day, using my technically superior broomstick putting, which takes the small muscles out of the stroke.

I can teach you how to ingrain a consistent, near-flawless stroke. If you start the ball off on the correct line and speed, you should be able to sink putts from within a 6-foot circle most every time. Long putts will be easier with fewer variables to be concerned with—such as wrist cock, flinching, pushing, pulling or adrenalin rushes.

Along with dramatically improving your lag putting, you'll make a lot more 15-30 footers and occasionally 30-60 footers! I teach my students nine critical putting keys for a near-perfect pendulum stroke, and sink putts from 10 feet or less, 90 percent of the time. (For a video of my putting skills and testimonials from students see **JeffGoldGolf.com**.)

CHAPTER 17

THE JOYS OF LIVING AND PLAYING GOLF IN MINNESOTA

Y ou've probably noticed I use the word *hell* every so often, and revere the devil now and then. But I want make it clear that I'm not a devil worshipper, but a sun worshipper who has become an Arizona Sun Devil. It sure beats being a Minnesota Gopher! What possessed some idiot to choose a rodent as the University of Minnesota's mascot?

My feeling is that here's nothing blasphemous about saying hell as it's just a name for a very old fictitious place. It's a fitting term for my vocabulary because as an avid golfer, living through Minnesota winters can be a living hell. Case in point, one night in January, a polar bear was pounding on my door and pleading with me to let him in because he was freezing to death! Admittedly, though, I was drinking heavily that night just to keep warm as my thrifty wife insisted on keeping the thermostat at 65 degrees.

Winter driving in Minnesota is dangerous, as my friend Bette knows. Her car slid off an icy road and slammed into a giant oak tree—in *April!* This sweet woman wound up totaling her brand-new Honda Accord. It was the deluxe model with heated seats—they come in mighty handy in frigid Minnesota. They're worthless if you live in the Phoenix area—as I do now.

To Minnesotans reading this book, you have my deepest sympathy. To readers who've never visited Minnesota in the summer time, you'll love our state bird—the mosquito. Through precise calculations, I've determined that if there are 100 mosquitoes on the golf course I'm playing, I'll wind up with exactly 100 mosquito bites on my head, neck, arms and legs by end of the round.

As if mosquitos aren't pesky enough, there are insects by the zillions living in Minnesota during summer which are even worse than mosquitoes. They're practically invisible, hence their name—no-see-ums. You don't see the damn things land on you, but you feel pin pricks all over your body throughout your round of golf. You don't notice the bites at first, but they swell up like little balloons the next day.

The loveliest feature of many of the courses in Minnesota, however, is snow storms in the middle of summer. At least it seems that way with thousands of cottonwood trees in full bloom releasing zillions of cottony allergens all over the golfers, putting surfaces, etcetera on the courses which they inhabit—driving allergy sufferers bonkers and vainly wishing, year after year, that (one day) every last one of those offensive trees will be cut down.

If you ask me what's the best time of year for a golfer in Minnesota, I'd say anytime you get the hell out of that god-forsaken state, and down as far south as you can get from the land of 10 zillion potholes—there you have it, yet, another reason for hating Minnesota.

If you're looking for a state with quality municipal courses, Minnesota's not for you. Most of the state's muni courses were designed by the lowest bidder who knew nothing about golf architecture. The strict mandates require that he have a bulldozer in working order and understand that greens should be void of grass and as hard as concrete, or muddy and unputtable during the rainy season.

Ironically, to play golf year-round on courses that are green and lush, I wound up moving to the Arizona desert where it rarely rains and is hotter than hell three months out of the year. Some people think we have four or five months of unbearably hot weather. But a superbly conditioned athlete like myself would never admit to being such a wimp.

Chapter 18

HOW GOLF AND THE BIBLE
ARE INTERCONNECTED

In regard to the Bible, one thing I've never figured out is how it was possible for Eve to have been created from Adam's rib—a thought of having a rib torn or cut out of one's body is insanely repulsive, in my view, not to mention terribly degrading to all of the women in this world!! For crying out loud, it's bad enough that women (to this day) are not allowed to become members at Augusta National! Furthermore, I don't want to even attempt to imagine how horrifically painful it would be to have a rib torn out of my body!!

However, having a serious disability such as that would explain why it took so long for Adam to win his first Major—ironically, at Augusta National. I happened to be there for the Masters in 2013 and was happy to see a fellow broomstick putter user win the playoff—though I feel quite certain that Adam's putting would improve after a lesson from me. For one thing, it would help if he stood up taller—with the ball closer to his feet. But that's the only putting tip I'm giving you, Adam—for free.

During that week, I followed Cabrera around a bit and witnessed him slamming his club on the ground a few times, after hitting a shot he wasn't happy with—albeit not one-tenth as hard as I slam my clubs. Nevertheless, as far as I'm concerned, Cabrera's no Angel.

In terms of religious beliefs (as they relate to golf) I try think logically, but also do my best to be open minded. For instance, I totally understand why Jesus never helps me out when I shout his name on the golf course as that would provide me with an unfair advantage over the rest of the field. It does, however, seem a bit unfair the way that Jesus went to extraordinary lengths in helping Bubba win his first Major—a fact that Bubba readily admitted to. And it happened at Augusta National, OF ALL PLACES.

Frankly, it was ridiculously obvious that Jesus intervened on that 170 yard wedge shot Bubba hit to within 10 feet of the pin (on the playoff hole) where Rossie (had he been alive) would have been quick to tell us that Bubba was in jail and had NO shot!! Besides that, I'm pretty sure it's physically impossible for any human to hit a gap wedge 170 yards! For crying out loud, Jesus, if you're going to provide a golfer with an unfair advantage, please don't make it so obvious!! In any case, I believe I've provided you with irrefutable evidence that Jesus does, in fact, exist. Besides that, Bubba tells me so.

If anyone knows, Bubba would, as Jesus helped him once again in winning his second Major—and once again at Augusta National!! Here again, it was only too obvious that Jesus was helping Bubba, as I can't believe that the drive I saw Bubba hit over the trees on the 13th hole Sunday (that left him with a mere flip wedge to the green—on a fricken par-5, for crying out loud!) was humanly possible. Now it's all becoming quite clear to me that Jesus (or at least his spirit), obviously, has made Augusta National his home. And it makes all the sense in the world. If I were Jesus (a bit of a stretch), hands down, I too would have chosen the home of the Masters as the place for my spirit to reside.

In Bubba's case, I highly doubt he'll ever win a third Masters. Reason being: I don't think Jesus could, in good conscience, help Bubba win his third Masters when there are sooo many other golfers out there who are just dying to win their first Green Jacket. I'm also thinking there's no way, on earth, Bubba could win the Master's without Jesus's help. Actually, I won't feel sorry for the guy if he winds up winning a total of only two Masters in his career. I'd love to win just one. Admittedly, it's probably a bit late for me. I wonder how many shots Jesus is willing to help me with per side. I'll, obviously, have to consult with Jesus on that one.

I find it hard not to love Jesus. As far as I'm concerned, any savior who is so big into golf that his spirit resides at Augusta National and is happy to help a loyal follower win a Masters title, not only once but twice, is a super cool guy. Also, I just figured out why Jesus didn't bother helping me out when I shouted his name—it was because, unlike Bubba at Augusta National, I was merely playing on a stupid dog track course in Minnesota.

The only thing that would make me an even stronger believer in Jesus would be to witness his second coming—as a living being, rather than just a spirit. But admittedly, I'm losing a little patience after waiting 50+ years. Nevertheless, it would be quite a thrill to see him play a round of golf. I'm thinking that he could probably will the ball into the hole—on every tee shot—making all of the PGA Tour players look like hackers!! Although I've never actually seen Jesus, I have played with golfers who were so slow it was akin to waiting for the second coming of Christ.

With this preponderance of evidence, I believe I have proven conclusively that golf and the Bible are interconnected. Also, it is my belief that Jesus has a wonderful sense of humor—after all, he's had over 2000 years to perfect it. By this time, he's, undoubtedly, put together one truly hilarious stand-up routine. I'm thinking that if the Augusta National members would (simply) listen closely enough, they could probably hear Jesus whispering jokes to them. The only problem is that most the members there are so old, they're probably as deaf as a fricken stone!

Whether or not you're a Christian, you have to concede that Bubba's belief in a higher power gave him the self-assurance, inner peace and mental strength that was needed by a guy with an unorthodox, home-made golf swing to achieve greatness. Any way you look at it, Jesus was instrumental to his winning two Master's Championships in a three year period.

It's interesting to me how Bubba has gone 2 for 2 in winning Masters titles when in or near the lead, heading into the final round. Whereas Greg Norman went zero for 6 (in the years 1981, 1986, 1987, 1995, 1996 and 1999) under similar circumstances. Not to be judgmental but could that be because Greg is a non-believer and had nothing to fall back on for comfort and inspiration while under intense pressure? I'm guessing that if Bubba had been in Norman's shoes, on all six of those occasions, he would have won at least four Green Jackets.

Interestingly, Larry Mize is also a man of strong faith and even a Christian speaker. Wasn't he the guy who beat Greg in the '87 Masters playoff with that miracle shot? Lacking strong faith can be mighty costly to a pro golfer—particularly at Augusta National. If you'd like further proof of this contention, simply look to Tiger. Since his adulterous sex scandal broke out, he's had nothing but bad (if not vicious) breaks at his former stomping ground—unless you call hitting a perfect wedge shot that strikes the flagstick and bounces into the water hazard a good break.

ACTION STEPS FOR GOLFERS

Action Step 1
Demand a retraction from *Golf Magazine,* with threat of boycott, for its ruthless mischaracterization of Johnny McDermott.

In light of the great golfing legend McDermott was, I urge you to send an email to the publisher of *Golf Magazine,* demanding a retraction of its terrible mischaracterization of McDermott by writer John Garitty, in the May 2, 2012, issue.

McDermott was described as "a famously rude, combative, abrasive, embarrassing, insane bigot, best left forgotten." This was a vicious attack on a very nice young man who was golf's first American hero.

Send email to Jon Tuck, associate publisher of Time, Inc., jon_tuck@timeinc.com. Mention *Golf's Forgotten Legends* in your email, so *Golf Magazine* readers can read the *true* story of Johnny McDermott.

Action Step 2

Demand that every bunker on Whistling Straits is equipped with a rake by 2015, like every other respectable course, and spectators are prohibited from trampling through or standing in any of its thousand bunkers, like every other tournament.

I urge you to call and write to The PGA of America and make these demands, so the bunker debacles in the PGA Championships of 2004 and 2010 will never happen again. Send your letters to: The PGA of America, 100 Avenue of the Champions, Palm Beach Gardens, FL 33418. Call (561) 624-8400.

Action Step 3

Demand the USGA immediately change Rule 33-7.

See my website, JeffGoldgolf.com, for a copy of the following petition.

Mike Davis
Director
USGA
Box 708
Far Hills, NJ 07931

Dear Mr. Davis,

I am among golf enthusiasts joining Jeff Gold, author of *Golf's Forgotten Legends,* to petition the USGA to make a drastic change to USGA Rule 33-7.

In no other sport can a participant be disqualified, after his competition has concluded, due to an innocent mistake on his part that occurred during the course of play. Any rules infraction during the course of play should be addressed by either the player, one of the playing partners, or a rules official, before the scorecard is signed by the player and the scorer.

The only people who should be able to call a penalty on a player are the player himself, one of his playing partners, or a rules official. If there is a rules violation dispute during the round, it should be settled before the scorecard is signed. If neither the player, nor one of his playing partners, nor an official notices any rules violation during the round, it should be too late for a player whose scorecard is signed to be penalized.

If a rules violation is observed during the course of play, there is plenty of time for the violation to be addressed before the scorecard is signed. It's unfair for a player to be disqualified, after signing his scorecard, for committing a minor violation of which he was unaware.

This simple rules change holds rules officials responsible for doing their job. When a player commits a violation and no one in the group, nor any officials on the scene, notices the infraction, it tends to be a minor violation that provided the player with no advantage over the rest of the field.

There have been numerous instances on the PGA Tour when players were disqualified after TV viewers phoned in to do the job rules officials were supposed to do. With this rules change, officials will be held accountable, and players will never again be severely punished with disqualification because officials were sleeping on the job.

Allowing the home TV viewer to call in and assess penalties gives the impression that rules officials not doing their job is acceptable. There is no other sport in which a TV viewer can call a penalty on a player. Why is golf the only sport in which this nonsense is allowed? It's high time the rules and penalty assessments in golf fall in line with other sports. This rules change should have been done with the elimination of stymies.

The rules change also would not allow players, trying to do the honorable thing, to disqualify themselves for some minor infraction they unknowingly committed the day before. It's stupid to penalize someone who is honest and reward someone who is not.

With this rules change, we will restore the responsibility of penalty enforcement and assessment where they belong—with the player, his playing partners and rules officials.

Respectfully,
(your name)

Action Step 4
Demand a ban on smoking at all PGA Tour events.

Jumbo, what a wonderful image you portray to the youngsters of Japan knowing that cigarette smoking causes so many terrible health disorders, including lung cancer, emphysema, pulmonary fibrosis, heart disease, throat cancer, bladder cancer, birth defects, diabetes, ectopic pregnancy, sinus trouble, rheumatoid arthritis, cervical cancer, prostate cancer, breast cancer, liver cancer and loss of vision.

Here we have the great Jumbo Ozaki

Shouldn't professional golfers be held to the same standards as athletes in every other sport and be prohibited from smoking during tournament competition? I concede that the PGA Tour has come a long way and there are very few smokers among the group. Nevertheless, there are still a few black sheep who think they're living back in the early 1960s, when smoking by tour pros was acceptable.

John Daly is possibly the worst chain-smoking offender who has done a great job of giving pro golfers a bad name. Tournament directors in Australia had enough sense to ban him from competition. John still has a fairly good-size following in the U.S., but Americans are big NASCAR fans and love watching car crashes. Daly fans are assured of witnessing a train wreck. John keeps his fans guessing when it may happen, on the first hole or second.

On the other hand, Daly's one of those guys who is liable to double cross me and start playing some good golf again. John better pray the smoking ban I'm spearheading doesn't materialize. But I recall Daly attended college at Satan's School for Boys; although he was expelled. From a conversation with Golf Australia's director of tournaments, Trevor Herden, he was not surprised John was too much for even Satan to handle. Trevor went so far as to suggest that Daly was the devil himself. Actually, the phrase Herden used was, "The devil who lost his balls."

John was a fool to pack it up in the 2011 Australian Open with the lame excuse that he ran out of golf balls, when he had a great chance of breaking Tommy Armour's legendary high score of 23 on a single hole. Trevor made it clear he would have gladly shared his balls with Daly.

The PGA Tour should be embarrassed that the LPGA Tour has been smoke-free for quite some time. Are these ladies better athletes than the men? I certainly wouldn't consider a smoker a well-conditioned athlete.

The time has come to ban smoking by PGA Tour players in tournament competition—this includes the Ben Hogan Tour (I still call it that), The PGA Tour and The Champions Tour. The ban should include all caddies and spectators, as well.

I urge you to contact PGA Tour National Headquarters to voice your strong support of this proposal. Here is their address and phone number. **PGA TOUR National Headquarters, 100 PGA TOUR Boulevard, Ponte Vedra Beach, FL 32082; (904) 285-3700**

Notice to PGA Tour National Headquarters: If you start receiving lots of calls from various sounding voices, all with a South African accent, 10 will get you 20 that it's Gary Player calling—Gary's a huge supporter of a smoking ban. Every call from Gary should count as 100 calls from mere mortals.

ACKNOWLEDGMENTS

I appreciate Tom Lehman's support of this project as he is such a golf legend in Minnesota and I understand that the Minneapolis Knights of Columbus chapter will soon be knighting him Sir Tom Lehman. No one from Minnesota is more deserving of that honor than Tom (except for me, of course). Tom and I strongly agree that Minnesota is a great place to be *from*.

I should thank Mike Shea for being such a great sport—at least I hope he is. I don't care what they say (or I said) about Mike, he's an OK guy.

Many thanks to Tim Nicholls, of Count Yogi® Golf, LLC, for all the great material he provided me on the amazing Count Yogi—arguably the most talented golfer in the history of the game.

Finally, I wish to thank my thorough and careful editor, Elissa Cottle, of artfulbusinesswriting.com.

AFTERWORD

Buying *Golf's Forgotten Legends* you can feel especially good knowing that proceeds will go to a worthy cause—the Kevin Trudeau Defense Fund. I'm outraged my friend Kevin was given a 10-year prison sentence for selling a weight-loss book with some claims that may have been slightly exaggerated.

Was it Kevin's fault that certain overweight people who bought his book couldn't restrict themselves to a 500 calorie-a-day diet? For crying out loud, where was their willpower??

Kevin received no credit for his creativity. He was mighty clever to select a dead surgeon general to endorse his book. Kevin's judge neglected to consider that this particular surgeon general never disputed any endorsements that were attributed to him in the book about Kevin's weight-loss cures.

Kevin expressed an interest in collaborating with me, after he's out of the slammer, on a book discussing a new golf swing he dreamed up, guaranteed to enable every able-bodied person to shoot in the 60s for 18 holes on any regulation-length course—from the black tees (the blue tees would be too easy). That book should be ready for publication, roughly, 10 years from now.

When Kevin's lawyers were asked why they failed Kevin, they used the lame excuse that they were just practicing. I tried that excuse after a bad final round in the Minnesota State Amateur in the 1980s and it didn't go over very well.

Officials frowned on my dropping a second ball down every time, after hitting a bad shot in order to figure out what the hell I was doing wrong.

Kevin, old buddy, you do realize I was kidding about raising money for you, right? Unfortunately, I can't do that because if I raised money for *you*, I'd be taking away from my most favorite charity—*me*. You lucked out, though, that your prison is equipped with a nine-hole golf course. I'm sure it's bad, but it's bound to be better than Whistling Straits was to Dustin Johnson.

Fortunately for me, I've heard that Herb Kohler, Whistling Strait's owner, has a wonderful sense of humor. Herb should thank me for trashing his course because my readers, who play his layout for the first time, will have such low expectations it will be impossible for Whistling Straits not to impress them emensely—even if they lose all their balls on that treacherous track. If I'm lucky, Herb may even comp me a free round on his majestic course. But for crying out loud, Herb, please make sure every bunker I may hit my drive into has a rake—which, for me, means any bunker that's more than 300 yards past the tee box.

As we sadly approach the end of *Golf's Forgotten Legends*, I have my fingers crossed *Golf Magazine* will come through with that retraction about Johnny McDermott. I'd hate to be forced to cancel my subscription to a magazine for which I have past issues that go all the way back to the 1800s. My oldest issue of *Golf Magazine* is so ancient it refers to Old Tom Morris as golf's up-and-coming star.

However, there was some controversy concerning OT's long, scruffy beard and how it didn't comply with the clean-cut image the tour was striving to portray. The other issue they had with Old Tom is that he was so overweight and out of shape he was starting to look almost as bad as Lumpy. But how in the hell did they know about Tim Herron way back then?? I'm thinking that Nostradamus must have warned the golf world of Lumpy's coming in one of his prophecies—just like his foretelling of Hitler's arrival that was destined to bring a scourge upon the earth.

It's a shame, though, how Nostradamus warned us all of Adolph's coming and Lumpy's too, of course—yet, the world was prepared for neither Hitler's mass destruction nor Herron's massive consumption. Sadly, Lumpy has put scores of all-you-can-eat buffet restaurants out of business.

With the lives of so many bankrupt buffet restaurant owners in ruins and Lumpy's PGA Tour career heading in that same path, an intervention was critically needed. Thus, I deemed it necessary to use my tough love approach to motivate Lumpy to lose 60 pounds or more and gain a healthier lease on life while saving him from a similar tragic fate as poor Porky Oliver.

My ultimate goal for Tim is to see him slim down to the extent that he's able to lose his unflattering nickname. A slimmed down Lumpy would probably play better golf and might even have a chance of regaining his full-time Tour status. I wish you the best of luck, my friend, and have all the confidence in the world you can do it. Admittedly, though, I said the same thing about the Vikings winning the Super Bowl on four different attempts.

By the way, Tim, if you need extra help in your weight loss quest, I have some great news. Barnes & Noble is now offering incredible bargain pricing ($1.99) on the Best Selling book, *The Weight Loss Cure "They" Don't Want You to Know About*—by the highly esteemed author, Kevin Trudeau.

With that we conclude *Golf's Forgotten Legends & Unforgettable Controversies*. This book makes a great gift for all important occasions and the unimportant ones too. I hope you join me, and find fulfillment, in following through with the action steps I recommend (particularly the one to change Rule 33-7) to help right the wrongs of the golf world and make it a better place.

ABOUT THE AUTHOR

 Jeff Gold is an author of golf books and part-time golf instructor who moved to the Phoenix area, prior to spending most of his life in Minnesota. He won numerous golf competitions over the years before shifting his focus to writing, teaching and playing golf.

Jeff is passionate about physical fitness and has developed an intensive, golf-specific fitness routine—designed to strengthen the neck, back and core areas of the body. This has enabled him to stay injury-free at age 56, while playing several rounds of golf and hitting hundreds of practice balls at high-clubhead speeds every week.

Jeff is humble when speaking about his golfing ability. Besides a phenomenal putter, he is a prodigiously long driver of the golf ball, turning 7,000-yard layouts into pitch-and-putts. To learn more about Jeff and his work, go to **www.JeffGoldGolf.com**.

CPSIA information can be obtained at www.ICGtesting.com
Printed in the USA
BVOW04s1310220315

392564BV00005B/6/P